THE BDD BOOKS

Discovery

Explore behaviour using examples

Gáspár Nagy and Seb Rose

Foreword by Johanna Rothman

The BDD Books - Discovery

Explore behaviour using examples

Gáspár Nagy and Seb Rose

ISBN 978-1983591259

Published on: February 2018

Book website: http://bddbooks.com/discovery

Tweet This Book!

Please help Gáspár Nagy and Seb Rose by spreading the word about this book on Twitter!

The suggested hashtag for this book is #bddbooks.

Find out what other people are saying about the book by clicking on this link to search for this hashtag on Twitter:

#bddbooks

Contents

Foreword

by Johanna Rothman

As a consultant, I see agile projects in trouble. Why? Because the requirements mean one thing to one person and another thing to other people. The team, the product owner, the business people – all of them have a different perspective on what the requirements are and what they mean.

Those people need this book.

In my 40+ years of experience, I've heard, "We'll know what's in here once we ship." Or, "It's not done if the whole thing isn't done." Or, "Let's get the bones of this requirement in and refine it later."

Those sayings weren't horrible. However, I've seen teams veer off in various directions that the customers didn't want or need, or that the product manager/owners didn't want. These teams (and others) suffered from the same problem: We didn't have examples to understand the requirements.

When we have examples, we – all of us, team members, product owners, business people, managers of all stripes – can discuss the reality of the work. Without examples, we flounder. Worse, we don't just delay the delivery of valuable features, we even implement the wrong work. We don't receive feedback early enough.

This book can change that for you. By defining the *behaviours* of your product, by creating, refining and using examples, your team can get faster feedback and deliver the product your customers need.

Gáspár and Seb guide you through thinking and practicing the Discovery part of BDD in this book: how to discover the requirements. They explain how Discovery is followed by Formulation (turning the examples into scenarios) and Automation (using the scenarios to test the behaviour).

It sounds easy to say. It's challenging to do, only because we often don't think of doing these three steps in this order.

One of the problems I see in teams is that, too often, the Product Owner (or some responsible person) is an order-taker from other people. The PO doesn't always understand the requirement itself. BDD can help expose that problem through the collaborative conversations.

Or, sometimes, the team is supposed to be like a short-order cook, taking the requirements from the PO without conversations. That rarely works, and this book has an entire chapter on how to build the requirements through conversations.

Some of my clients are a little stuck on rules, examples, acceptance criteria and how to use them properly. Gáspár and Seb devote one chapter to explaining what the examples are and how to frame them. I appreciate the positive way of structuring examples, even on the paths you want to prevent people from exploring in your product.

There's a chapter that addresses who does what and when. Because agile approaches are a system, it's not a flow chart – Gáspár and Seb created a diagram that shows how the various practices that make up the BDD approach interact. They emphasize that business review of the team's work is needed and clarify how BDD practices tie into implementation and refactoring. They also explain how you might have additional tests and when you might release.

The last chapters discuss how to use BDD in almost any project – not just agile approaches – and how to involve your business partners.

Read this book to start using BDD effectively. You, your team, your customers and your managers will all be glad you did. I can't wait for the next book!

Johanna Rothman

consultant, author, and speaker

Arlington, Massachusetts

Preface

Behaviour Driven Development (BDD) is an agile approach to software development that insists that detailed requirements for a feature should be defined collaboratively by the business and delivery teams. The output of this collaboration is documented using business terminology that can be understood unambiguously. Finally, the documentation is structured in a way that enables it to act as automated tests that verify that the system behaves as intended. This book explores, in detail, the collaborative aspect of BDD.

BDD has been proven to be successful in thousands of projects around the world, on different platforms, in diverse industries and various project sizes. BDD is based on a set of practices that originate from the experience of many people over many years, working to *uncover better ways of delivering software.* However, there is a learning period (or more accurately, a practicing period) for BDD, so it will take some time before you start seeing a return on your investment.

We belong to the second generation of the software industry (we could call ourselves Generation Y - there are a lot of similarities). We don't believe in buzzwords or well-named methodologies, but we like to try them out to see if they work. So, if you try out BDD, how can you decide if it has worked or not?

The first indicator you are likely to notice is a reduction in ***cycle time***. The shared understanding that is gained during collaborative requirement definition sessions ensures a smooth flow from definition to delivery. If a developer or a tester discovers an ambiguity in a requirement once they have started working on it, they'll need to resolve it. This interrupts their work, as well as the work of any colleague that they ask to help. The elimination of interruptions and context switches leads to a more efficient, more predictable delivery process.

Another visible indicator is a reduction in the number of production issues. Although it is very hard to gather scientific evidence of this (because it is hard to find a "control project"), we have seen significantly fewer production issues in projects that have successfully adopted a BDD approach. For a broad review of outcomes, from a wide variety of teams, you can't do better than reading Gojko Adzic's "Specification By Example" [1].

BDD helps preserve the quality and maintainability of the software, so a further indicator is that the implementation costs of new features is kept low. This is in contrast to many other projects where, as the codebase grows, the cost of adding (or modifying) a feature increases exponentially. If allowed to deteriorate in this way, your project will finally reach the point where it is not possible to add new features anymore in a cost-efficient way and people will start talking about a "rewrite".

Our goal with this book is to ease your way through the learning period, avoiding the mistakes that we made while we were learning.

One typical mistake is to see BDD as a tool-thing. BDD is primarily about collaboration and domain discovery; any "BDD tool" can be only useful in supporting this process. You have to start by investing in collaborative discussions and the creation of a shared vocabulary. Just going after automation (using Cucumber or SpecFlow) does not work.

It doesn't.

Honest.

As we said, we don't believe in buzzwords, but if you intend to evaluate the BDD approach objectively, it is important to do it at full throttle during the evaluation period. You might feel uncomfortable or skeptical when you start doing BDD (like with any other new approach). That is absolutely fine, but don't let the evaluation be hampered by your fears. Once you have decided to evaluate how BDD could work for your team, give yourself enough time to get comfortable with the approach. Try, as far as possible, to follow our recommendations.

You're at the beginning of a brave new world. Let us help you to explore that world and discover the benefits that are waiting.

---

[1]Adzic, Gojko. *Specification by Example: How Successful Teams Deliver the Right Software.* Shelter Island, NY: Manning, 2011. Print.

Who this book is for

This book is written for everyone involved in the specification and delivery of software (including product owners, business analysts, developers and testers). The book starts by explaining the reasons that BDD exists in the first place and describes techniques for getting the most out of collaboration between the ***delivery team*** (those that implement the solution) and the ***business team*** (those that work on the requirements).

Just to re-iterate, this book is aimed at everyone involved in the project, irrespective of their role, whether they come from a software background or not.

It's also worth stressing that this book is tool agnostic. Whether you use Cucumber, SpecFlow, JBehave, Fit, FITNESSE, RSpec, Jasmine, Behave, or any other BDD tool – this book will help your team collaborate.

Why you should listen to us

Gáspár is the creator and main contributor of SpecFlow, the most widely used ATDD/BDD framework for .NET.

He is an independent coach, trainer and test automation expert focusing on helping teams implementing BDD and SpecFlow through his company, called Spec Solutions. He has more than 15 years of experience in enterprise software development as he worked as an architect and agile developer coach.

He shares useful BDD and test automation related tips on his blog (http://gasparnagy.com) and on Twitter (@gasparnagy). He edits a monthly newsletter (http://bddaddict.com) about interesting articles, videos and news related to BDD, SpecFlow and Cucumber.

Seb has been a consultant, coach, designer, analyst and developer for over 30 years. He has been involved in the full development lifecycle with experience that ranges from Architecture to Support, from BASIC to Ruby.

During his career, he has worked for companies large (e.g. IBM, Amazon) and small, and has extensive experience of failed projects. He's now a partner in Cucumber Limited, who help teams adopt and refine their agile practices, with a particular focus on collaboration and automated testing.

He's a regular speaker at conferences, a contributing author to "97 Things Every Programmer Should Know" (O'Reilly) and the lead author of "The Cucumber for Java Book" (Pragmatic Programmers).

He blogs at cucumber.io and tweets as @sebrose.

Together Seb and Gáspár have over 50 years of software experience.

Acknowledgements

This book would not have been possible without the help of our reviewers:

- Gojko Adzic
- Garret Burns
- Darren Cauthon
- Lisa Crispin
- Claude Hanhart
- Dave Hanlon
- Sam Holder
- Alexandra Fung
- Adrienn Kolláth
- Gilbert Liddell
- Viktor Nemes
- Paul Rayner
- Chuck Suscheck
- Steve Tooke
- Andreas Willich

How this book series is organised

This is the first of the BDD Books series, that will guide you through the end-to-end adoption of BDD, including specific practices needed to successfully drive development using collaboratively authored specifications and living documentation.

Once you've implemented the approach we described you can read:

- Formulation (Book 2): express examples using Given/When/Then[2]
- Automation with SpecFlow (Book 3)[3]

What is not in this book

- Formulation
- Structuring documentation
- Gherkin
- Tools
- Automation
- Code

Online resources

http://bddbooks.com

Gáspár Nagy and Seb Rose, August 2017

[2]Nagy, Gáspár, and Seb Rose. *The BDD Books: Formulation.* In preparation. http://bddbooks.com/formulation.

[3]Nagy, Gáspár, and Seb Rose. *The BDD Books: Automation with SpecFlow.* In preparation. http://bddbooks.com/specflow.

Chapter 1 – What is BDD?

Behaviour Driven Development (BDD) is an agile approach to delivering software that has been gaining momentum over the past ten years, or so. In this chapter, we take a look at why BDD came into existence, what challenges it addresses and take a high level look at how it works.

> **Seb's story: BDD, ATDD or Specification By Example?**
>
> I used to get confused by all the different names that I read in blog posts. There was Behaviour Driven Development (BDD), Acceptance Test-Driven Development (ATDD) and Specification By Example. I tried to work out how they differed, but eventually I realised (helped by Liz Keogh[a]) that they were just different names for the same thing.
>
> [a]http://lizkeogh.com/2011/06/27/atdd-vs-bdd-and-a-potted-history-of-some-related-stuff/

1.1 – The missing link

The purpose of software development is to deliver solutions to business problems. A continuing challenge is to verify that the software actually satisfies the requirements. Waterfall methods had slow feedback cycles built into them, allowing projects to go seriously off track. In response, the industry began to experiment with lightweight methodologies like XP and Scrum.

Agile iterations are often mis-implemented as mini-waterfalls. Teams spend weeks implementing a user story. *After* that comes testing, to make sure they got it right. When they discover a mistake, they have to fix the problem and retest the story –

a tedious and time-consuming process. The resulting delay in feedback continues to limit the benefits that agile development methods can deliver.

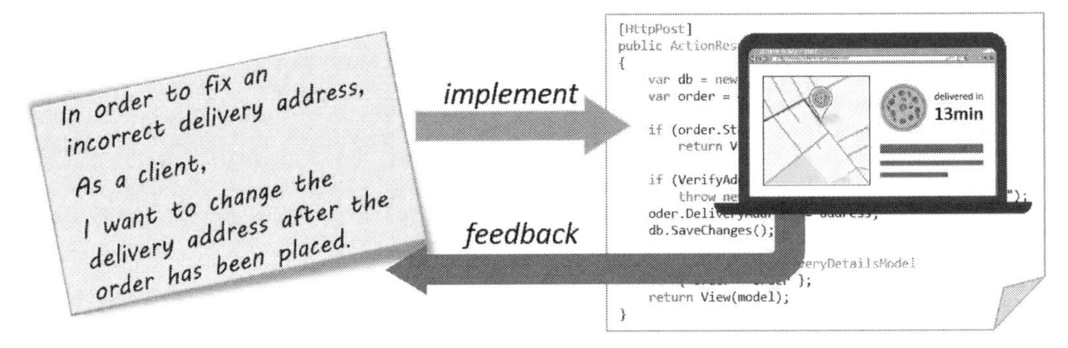

Figure 1 – Agile mini-waterfall

Test-Driven Development (TDD) helps speed up the feedback loop by demanding that teams write automated tests *before* they write the code. That in itself is not enough.

Gaspar's story: Automation is not enough

In a company I was working for, testing new features was always chaotic. We never did any testing until after the feature was *done* and it was only then that we discovered we had misunderstood things had previously seemed *obvious*. Unfortunately, since this testing was all manual, things did not get any better after this. We continued to need real people, running through test scripts, to make sure that the application still behaved as expected. Tedious, manual regression testing.

We needed automation - this is how we wanted to improve the regression testing problem. However, automating our scripts required us to write code, and the code became hard to follow, even for other developers. This created a barrier to having discussions about misunderstandings and different interpretations of *obvious*. We needed a solution that made tests automatable, but preserved their connection to requirements.

In the early days, **JUnit** required developers to use the word "test" in their method names and this overemphasised one goal of unit tests ("testing") at the expense of other goals, such as design, documentation, and definition of the expected behaviour. By giving them a name like `OrderTest`, they become detached from the business requirement as soon as the test has been completed. And as time goes by, this gap gets bigger and bigger.

Dan North noticed this problem and suggested some practical rules for naming and structuring the test methods to preserve their connection with the requirements.[4] He also explained that the easiest way to verify whether our tests expressed the expected behaviour was to show them to the business representatives. However, business people rarely read source code, so he developed a small tool that performed a few simple transformations to make the test results business-readable.

He called this concept ***Behaviour Driven Development*** (BDD)[5], intentionally removing the word "test" to encourage business people to remain engaged throughout the process. BDD helps maintain a connection between the requirements and the software – and as such acts as a bridge. Gojko Adzic even called his first book "Bridging the communication gap" [6].

The bridge is made out of *examples*. Every test is an example. Each example is an expression of a required system behaviour. If you have sufficient examples you define the behaviour of the system - you have documented the requirements. Business people remain engaged, because the examples are expressed in business language. Fast feedback is preserved, because the examples are automated.

These examples are often written using the ***Given***, ***When*** and ***Then*** keywords (introduced by Chris Matts[7]) and called ***scenarios***:

[4]Similar problems had been observed by other people, such as Kent Beck with Customer Tests ("Extreme Programming Explained: Embrace Change"), Joshua Kerievsky https://www.industriallogic.com/blog/storytest-driven-development-article/, Ward Cunningham (http://fit.c2.com/) and Eric Evans ("Domain-driven Design: Tackling Complexity in the Heart of Software")

[5]https://dannorth.net/introducing-bdd/

[6]Adzic, Gojko. *Bridging the Communication Gap: Specification by Example and Agile Acceptance Testing.* London: Neuri, 2009. Print.

[7]https://theitriskmanager.wordpress.com/about/

```
Scenario: Allow address change while the order is in preparation
  Given the client's order is currently 'in preparation'
  When the client changes the delivery address
  Then the change should be accepted
  And the new address should be set as the delivery address
```

The scenarios represent the requirement details and they are formal enough to be executed by a computer, to give feedback about the implementation. Teams sometimes write their own tools to support this, but there are several freely available *BDD tools* that make this simple, such as **SpecFlow**[8] and **Cucumber**[9].

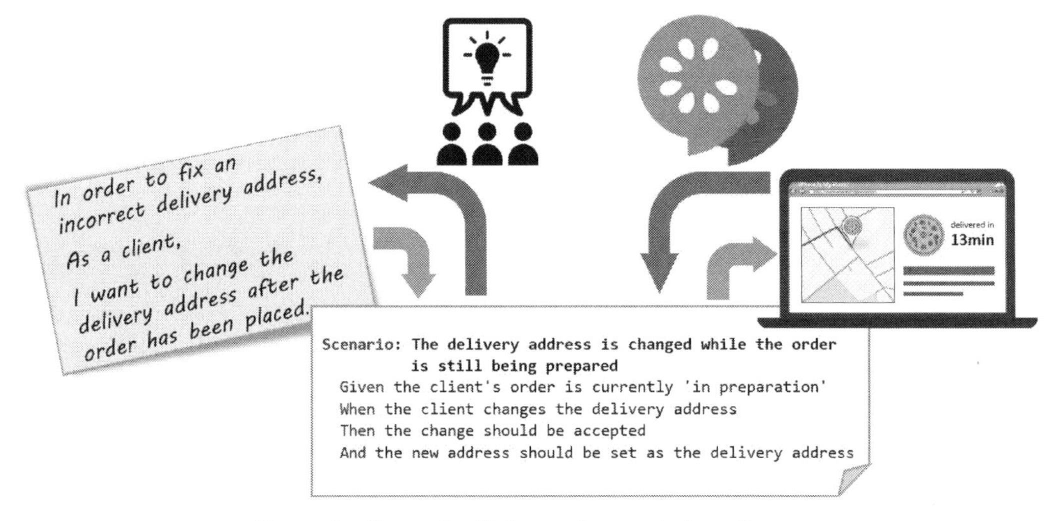

Figure 2 – Scenarios link requirements to software

The bridge built with the examples has been ignored by software developers for decades.[10] Agile itself didn't address this directly, but BDD does. As Matt Wynne said[11], "BDD can save your agile." In short, BDD is the missing link.

[8]http://www.specflow.org

[9]http://cucumber.io

[10]Brian Marick was an early exponent of examples http://www.exampler.com/old-blog/2003/08/22/#agile-testing-project-2

[11]https://www.youtube.com/watch?v=ReEkLYoXjK8

1.2 – How does BDD work?

Examples (and their formalized representation - scenarios) play a critically important role in BDD. To understand how BDD works, let's have a look at the way that these scenarios are created and how they drive the development process.

Behaviour Driven Development is typically used in agile projects, the requirements are discovered using user stories that the team discusses throughout the project. Defining and prioritizing good user stories is an exciting challenge in itself. There are many good methods you can use, like impact mapping or story mapping, but these are not directly related to BDD and are therefore out of the scope of this book. BDD kicks in when the details of the user stories are discussed by the team for the first time (see Chapter 4, *Who does what and when*).

In a project following the BDD approach, we collect and discuss examples while working with a user story. We use the examples to explore and illustrate the expected behaviour of the business domain.

User stories are typically broken down into acceptance criteria or business rules, but these are often subject to misunderstandings. Focusing on examples makes the intention of these rules clear - each rule should be *illustrated* by one or more examples. However, examples also enable us to *explore* our understanding of a rule. Exploration often leads to the discovery of complexities and assumptions that otherwise would not be found until much later in the development process.

In Chapter 2, *Structured conversation*, we show in more detail what these examples look like and how you can facilitate requirement workshops to discover them. For now, let's say that examples are concrete usage descriptions of how the application or one of its features should behave. The better the examples you collect during the requirement workshop, the easier it will be to deliver the project successfully using BDD.

Examples can take various forms. They can appear as input-output data pairs, sketches of the user interface, bulleted lists of different steps of a user workflow or even an Excel workbook illustrating a calculation or a report. The only thing that is common to all examples is that they describe a behaviour as a combination of ***context***, ***action***, and ***outcome*** - which we'll describe in detail in Chapter 3, *What is an example?*.

Once the user story is prepared and discussed with the team, the development phase starts. Using BDD, teams implement the expected behaviour that was illustrated by the examples. In order to use the examples to drive the development, we ***formulate*** some of them into scenarios. The scenarios can be considered part of the code base of the application, because they are used to verify a specific version of the application. BDD tools turn these scenarios into executable tests *before* the related behaviour has been implemented in the application itself.

Seb's story: Formulation

When I first started working with Gáspár, I wondered why he kept using the word "formulate". It's not a term used by software professionals in general, or BDD practitioners in particular. He explained that it was the best word that he had found to describe the process of turning concrete examples into business-readable documentation. I was pretty sure there must be a better word, so I went away to try to think of one.

I tried substituting with "translate", but there's a lot of creative energy required to write a good BDD scenario. "Translate" didn't do it justice, and nor did "convert".

The Merriam_webster dictionary defines formulate as: *to put into a systematized statement or expression.* This is an accurate description of what we do when we convert examples into scenarios. This is an important task that is uniquely focused on by BDD practitioners and it deserves a precise name. *Formulation* is ideal!

With test-driven development (TDD), we drive the application development by writing a test first - one that initially fails. Then we implement the application so that the test passes. After a code cleanup (refactoring), we can move on to the next test. This cyclic development flow is illustrated in Figure 3.

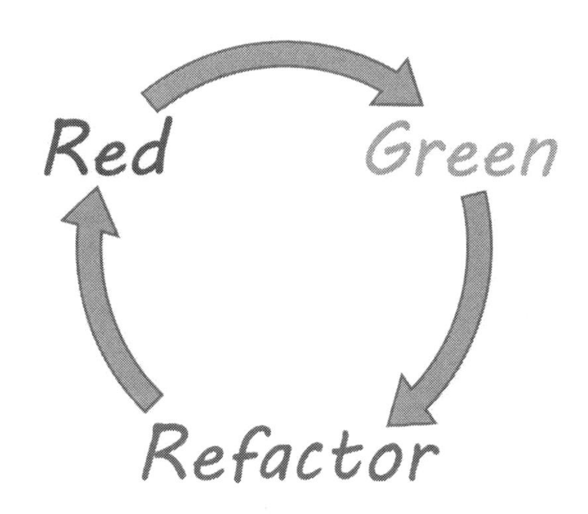

Figure 3 – The TDD cycle

BDD drives the development in a very similar way, although the scenarios are often expressed at a higher level. We start by writing a new scenario that should initially fail, then we iteratively implement the automation and application code until the scenario finally passes. After cleaning up the codebase (refactoring), we can move on to the next scenario.

BDD does not replace TDD (although Matt Wynne and Aslak Hellesøy defined BDD as "TDD done right" in the "Cucumber Book" [12]). Teams who use BDD often use TDD for ensuring the quality of the inner structure in the application. Figure 4 shows the BDD cycle and how it fits to the TDD loop (Freeman & Pryce: "Growing object-oriented software guided by tests" [13]).

[12] Wynne, Matt, and Aslak Hellesøy. *The Cucumber Book: Behaviour-driven Development for Testers and Developers.* Dallas, TX: Pragmatic helf, 2012. Print.

[13] Freeman, Steve, and Nat Pryce. *Growing Object-oriented Software Guided by Tests.* S.l.: Addison-Wesley Professional, 2009. Print.

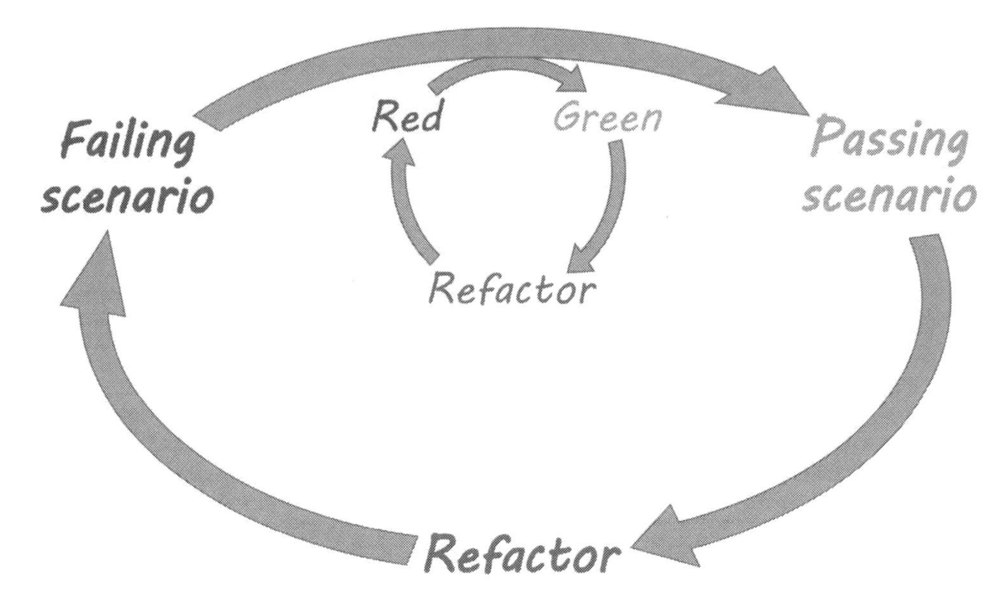

Figure 4 – The BDD cycle

An executable BDD scenario provides useful feedback for the entire team, including the business representatives.

- It gives feedback about the implementation correctness for the developers
- It gives feedback about the solution for the product owner
- It describes the implemented behaviour helping business analysts understand existing functionality
- It gives a signal for the manual, exploratory testers that a feature is ready for testing
- It provides a safety net for the developers, identifying any unwanted side-effects of changes
- It provides detailed documentation of the application for the support team
- It defines a domain language that is understood by everyone

1.3 – What about testing?

We mentioned earlier that the word "test" had been intentionally left out from the name of Behaviour Driven Development. The aim was to achieve a better engagement of business representatives. When first hearing about BDD, many testers have concerns about how it will affect their role, responsibilities, and position.

BDD does not replace classic testing and testing skills. In fact, BDD itself does not define how testing should be performed. Instead, it provides a set of practical guidelines that facilitate the *agile testing process*. Agile testing is described in detail in the book by Janet Gregory and Lisa Crispin, called "Agile Testing" [14]. The basic concept of agile testing is to move the responsibilities of testing from finding and reporting application issues to ensuring that these issues are never added to the codebase in the first place.

It's a little bit like the relationship between catching criminals and crime prevention. Crime prevention is a much nicer and cheaper way of ensuring security, but it does not replace the presence of police on the streets. The same happens with testing in a BDD project. Testers are involved in all project requirement discussions, to help *prevent* bugs. Later on, they will still work on verifying the correctness of the created product – *catching* bugs.

A significant proportion of defects[15] are rooted in problems that arise from misunderstood requirements. Misunderstandings can arise for many reasons: language barrier issues, unspecified combinations, ambiguous domain terms or different interpretations of common sense. Testers can help by pointing out inconsistencies, identifying examples or considering edge cases while a user story is being discussed. Testers can also give support in evaluating approaches to testing new features.

Not all defects are eliminated during these discussions. Verification remains critical, though it does become slightly different. Due to the high level of automation, less time is spent on manual regression testing and more on exploratory verification. The latter needs a much broader sense of correctness, which can be ensured only by a human. This kind of verification is usually done through ***exploratory testing*** (Elisabeth Hendrickson: "Explore It!" [16]).

The change of focus described above leads to better integration of testers into the team.

---

[14]Crispin, Lisa, and Janet Gregory. *Agile Testing: A Practical Guide for Testers and Agile Teams.* Upper Saddle River, NJ: Addison-Wesley, 2009. Print.

[15]J.-C. Chen and S.-J. Huang, "An empirical analysis of the impact of software development problem factors on software maintainability," Journal of Systems and Software, vol. 82, pp. 981-992 June 2009.

[16]Hendrickson, Elisabeth, Ward Cunningham, and Jacquelyn Carter. *Explore It! Reduce Risk and Increase Confidence with Exploratory Testing.* Dallas: Pragmatic helf, 2013. Print.

1.4 – A language that is understood by everyone

Robert C. Martin, alias Uncle Bob, has said that a software project cannot be successful without the dev team becoming domain experts at some level. You can write good software only for problems that you understand. Anything else works only for the short term. When you decided to work as an IT professional, you probably did not expect to need deep knowledge of heavy-duty construction equipment or sports event broadcasting. Whenever you join a project, you will certainly become familiar with its business domain. At the end of the day, this makes our job more interesting. We should see every project as a voyage of discovery.

Gaspar's story: Find the right words

I was renovating the roof of our terraced house and had to go to the plumbing shop to buy a few missing items. I knew what I needed, because I had already seen hundreds of gutters. Nevertheless, the first five minutes were spent explaining what I wanted and discovering what the name of that "thing" was. We even needed to draw some sketches. Once we agreed on what the "thing" I wanted was called, they could serve me quickly. It was even in stock!

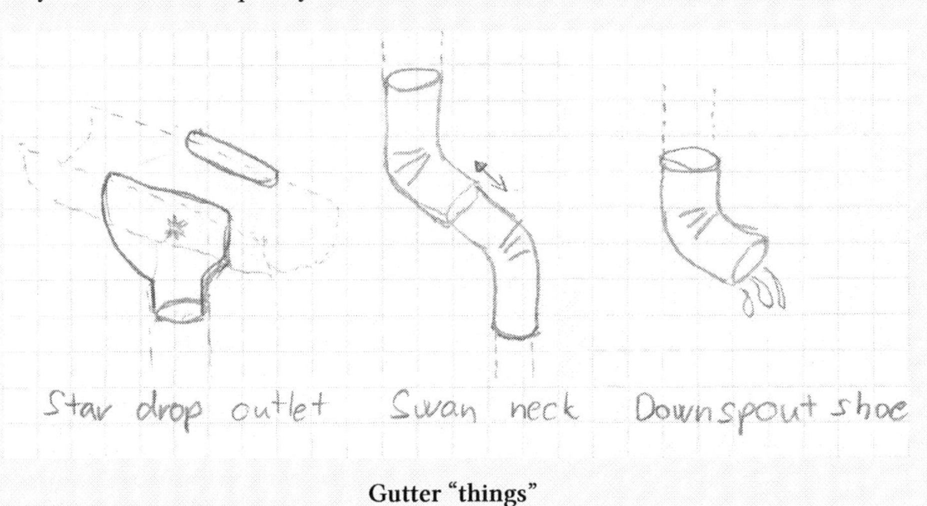

Gutter "things"

Software projects have the same challenges. A rough understanding of the project's business domain is usually not enough to provide a precise solution. We have to define a language in which the customer can explain their problems in detail and in which we also can explain the solution we are going to provide. A language that is understood by everyone. Eric Evans uses the term ***ubiquitous language***[17] for this in domain-driven design[18] (DDD).

The team writes scenarios using this language. If we use these scenarios to drive our implementation, the model we create for the solution will remain close to the business domain. This, in turn, helps keep our software easy to understand and maintain. In *The BDD Books: Formulation*[19] we talk more about the ubiquitous language and how to write scenarios that focus on the business domain.

1.5 – Living documentation

If you have heard about BDD, you have probably stumbled across the term ***living documentation***. This is a kind of documentation that never gets outdated, or at least you will be immediately informed when it does.

It is easy to see that the scenarios make up a kind of living structure, because we can always verify whether a scenario is supported by the application or not. If it is supported, the scenario passes. If not, the scenario fails. Thanks to the ubiquitous language, even the business representatives will immediately know which expectations may not be fulfilled by our solution.

It is harder to see how these scenarios can be used as a documentation. The target users of this kind of living documentation are the business representatives of the project and the development team (including testing, operations and support). Scenarios are written in a language that uses domain-specific terms to describe the behaviour of the application. As such, they are readable by, and interesting to, domain experts, but not necessarily for end users. Therefore, the scenarios are not a replacement for end user documentation or online help.

Scenarios are most useful when someone needs to check how the system works in some specific situations: "Is 'OR' search supported?", "Can our system handle zero

[17] http://martinfowler.com/bliki/UbiquitousLanguage.html

[18] Evans, Eric. *Domain-driven Design: Tackling Complexity in the Heart of Software.* Boston: Addison-Wesley, 2004. Print.

[19] Nagy, Gáspár, and Seb Rose. *The BDD Books: Formulation.* In preparation. http://bddbooks.com/formulation.

interest rate?", "What happens if multiple users attempt to change the same order?" We could answer these questions by trying them out on a test installation, but that might require complex setup steps that take a lot of time and effort. If you are planning a new feature and would like to know its impact on the system, or if you are on a support call, you can search for a few keywords in the living documentation. The scenarios found will describe the current behaviour of the system, providing you with the information you were looking for.

The success of using scenarios as living documentation mainly depends on whether you can make it accessible for the target audience in a convenient way. It is hard to imagine that a business analyst will open Visual Studio, do a git pull, find the scenarios that he or she is interested in and read them as plain text file. Fortunately there are several tools that can help with this, thanks to the Gherkin open specification format[20] used by the scenarios shown in this book. Make sure you check out **Cucumber Pro**[21], **Pickles**[22], **Relish**[23], **SpecFlow+ Runner**[24] and **SpecLog**[25] (to name a few).

1.6 – What is BDD, then?

BDD is an agile approach that consists of three practices that have to be addressed in order. The first practice is *discovery*, a structured, collaborative activity that uses concrete examples to uncover the ambiguities and misunderstandings that traditionally derail software projects.

The second practice is *formulation*, a creative process that turns the concrete examples produced during discovery into business-readable scenarios. The subsequent review of the scenarios delivers the confidence that the team really has understood what the business is asking for.

The third, and final, practice is *automation* where code is written that turns the scenarios into tests. The benefits of automation are many and various:

[20]https://github.com/cucumber/gherkin

[21]https://cucumber.io/pro

[22]http://www.picklesdoc.com/

[23]https://www.relishapp.com/

[24]http://www.specflow.org/plus/runner/

[25]http://www.speclog.net/

- when the tests pass, the development team can be confident they have delivered what the business have asked for
- the tests give the development team a safety net when the time comes to modify the code
- the tests form *living documentation* of how the system behaves, readable by the business, guaranteed to be up-to-date

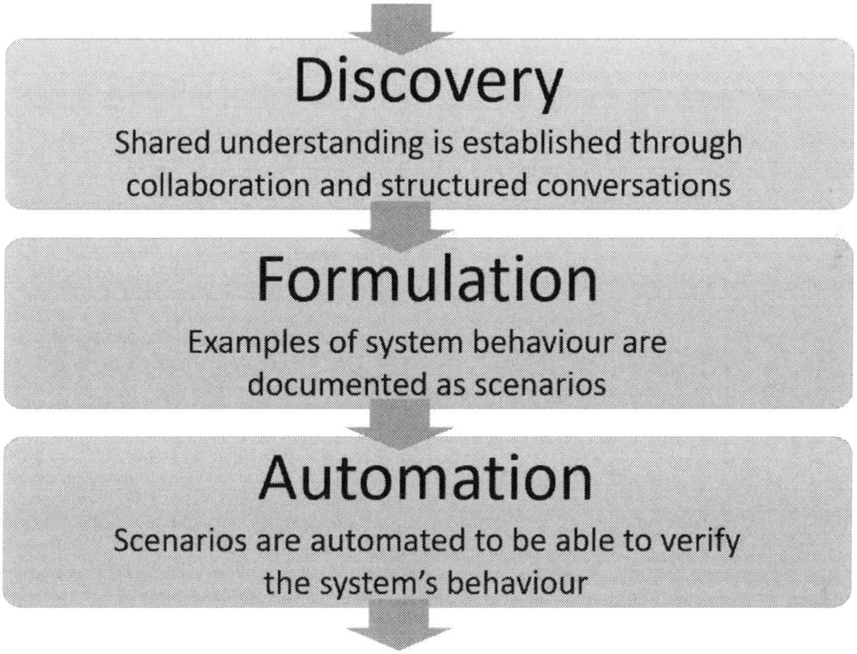

Discovery
Shared understanding is established through collaboration and structured conversations

Formulation
Examples of system behaviour are documented as scenarios

Automation
Scenarios are automated to be able to verify the system's behaviour

Figure 5 – BDD practices

Many development teams come to BDD through the desire to improve their test automation. Improved test automation **is** one of the significant outcomes of following a BDD approach, but it is a *downstream* outcome. Unless you adopt the practices in the order described (*discovery*, *formulation*, *automation*) you will not gain the expected benefits.

Conversely, you will achieve significant improvements in your software development activities just by practicing *discovery* on its own. Add *formulation* and you'll get the extra benefits that come from growing a truly ubiquitous language through an active review and feedback process.

And finally, creating an extra, business-language layer of automated tests is expensive – you'll only get a good return on your investment if you successfully engage the business team members. So, don't focus on the automation tools[26] until you've got good at collaborating across the team.

1.7 – What we just learned

In this chapter you've been on a whirlwind tour of BDD. There's a lot going on!

We started by describing the challenges that BDD was created to address – the failures caused by misunderstandings within a project team. We showed how examples (and the scenarios that we formulate from them) make an excellent bridge between business requirements and technical specifications, effectively flushing out ambiguities.

These scenarios, written in the project's ubiquitous language, act both as documentation and as tests. As documentation, they close the feedback loop between the business and delivery members, demonstrating the successful communication of ideas. As tests, they show that the solution being developed is meeting the business requirements, as well as acting as a valuable safety net that will provide confidence whenever changes need to be made to the software. Finally, once the scenarios are automated there's a further benefit – documentation that demonstrably describes the actual functionality provided by the software.

We also discussed the relationship between BDD and testing. They are related, but distinct. The focus of BDD is collaboration, leading to clear requirements understood by the whole team. The examples make great test cases and (once formulated) documentation – so there is definitely testing going on. However, the purpose is to assure all concerned that development is progressing in the correct direction, not to confirm exhaustively that the correct code has been written. This is still covered by the professional practices of developers and testers – developers writing automated programmer tests, testers verifying the solution using scripted and exploratory testing.

The rest of this book digs deeper into the collaborative, *discovery* practice – and how to fit it into your project's process.

---

[26]http://lizkeogh.com/2014/01/22/using-bdd-with-legacy-systems/

The next book, *The BDD Books: Formulation*[27], will examine the techniques and pitfalls of *formulation.*

Finally, the *The BDD Books: Automation with SpecFlow*[28] book will go into detail about the way an application can be *automated* with SpecFlow and gives in-depth examples of how to design maintainable automation code.

---

[27] Nagy, Gáspár, and Seb Rose. *The BDD Books: Formulation.* In preparation. http://bddbooks.com/formulation.

[28] Nagy, Gáspár, and Seb Rose. *The BDD Books: Automation with SpecFlow.* In preparation. http://bddbooks.com/specflow.

Chapter 2 – Structured conversation

In this chapter, we are going to peer into the daily work of a software product team to learn more about how they use structured conversations to help them discover what the expected behaviour of the next feature should be. We'll start by describing one of their requirement workshops. This will introduce concepts that you're not familiar with, but don't worry, all your questions will be answered later in the chapter.

2.1 – Where is my pizza?

The team we will be visiting is developing a pizza delivery management application for a large pizza company. The application will allow clients to track the real-time location of their order(s), so they have come up with a fun name for the application: "Where is my pizza?" Some joker on the team noticed that this abbreviates to WIMP – "a weak, cowardly, or ineffectual person" (Merriam-Webster). The rest of the team still know that the product will be awesome.

There are lots of other exciting features too, but for the rest of this book we'll be considering a client's ability to modify the delivery address of an order after the order has been submitted.

2.2 – A useful meeting

It's 9 a.m. on Wednesday morning and the team is assembling in the team room for another ***requirement workshop***. There's a good turnout today - Patricia (the PO), Dave and Dishita (from Development), Tracey (from Test) and Ian (the new intern).

Requirement workshop

The team meets regularly (usually several times a week) to discuss the work that they'll be undertaking in the next sprint or two. The purpose of this meeting is to explore a story, understand it's scope and illustrate it unambiguously with concrete examples. While they're doing this, they may discover new details about the story. They may also ask questions that no one at the meeting is able to answer right away.

What matters most in this meeting is to bring diverse perspectives together, so that they can learn about what needs to be done and work together more effectively. In other organizations, similar meetings have been variously called ***three amigos meeting***, ***discovery workshop***, ***specification workshop***, ***story refinement***, ***product backlog refinement*** and ***backlog grooming*** – as always, the name is less important than the purpose.

They're very comfortable with this meeting format, because they meet several times a week for short, focused sessions that often work only on a single user story. The idea came from a blog post by Matt Wynne Introducing Example Mapping[29] that Dishita had recently read.

Patricia grabs the box of colored index cards and marker pens from the stationery cupboard and puts them in the middle of the table. Everyone knows which story Patricia has been preparing because she sent out an email yesterday. Patricia reads out the story that is going to be discussed:

> In order to fix an incorrect delivery address,
>
> As a client,
>
> I want to be able to change the delivery address after the order has been placed.

Dishita summarizes this on a yellow index card:

[29]https://cucumber.io/blog/2015/12/08/example-mapping-introduction

Figure 6 – Story card on the table

“The system will need to be able to check whether it’s possible to change the delivery address”, says Patricia. “We’ll have to check that the new address is not too far from the current one. And we’ll need to check the state of the order too.” “This will be easy”, says Dave and they all smile. They have heard this sentence many times before. “We’ll see”, answers Tracey, “let’s try to come up with a few examples!” And the workshop begins.

> Explaining a team discussion in a book is hard, because you need to keep track of the goals and perspectives of many people with different roles and backgrounds. To make it easier to follow, we have chosen the names of our team members so that their initials describe their role. **P**atricia is the **P**roduct Owner, **D**ave and **D**ishita are **D**evelopers, **T**racey is a **T**ester and **I**an is an **I**ntern from the University.

As we mentioned in Section 1.6, *What is BDD, then?*, one typical mistake is to look at BDD as a tool-thing. A similar mistake would be to think of BDD as a mechanical process, such as filling out a *Given/When/Then* template. We need all team members to actively challenge their understanding of the user story by coming up with concrete examples.

There are many ways you can organize your team for better collaboration. Every team and every project is different. We are going to focus on a technique called ***Example Mapping*** that is a simple and efficient way to facilitate your requirement workshops. This is one technique for carrying out a structured conversation, and it has worked very well for us, but you may need to find an alternative that is more suited to your context. Before you do, refer to Chapter 4, *Who does what and when*, where we will show how requirement workshops can fit into an agile project following Scrum, Lean/Kanban or even into a fixed scope project with distributed teams.

So let's get back to our team…

2.3 – Collecting examples

"Let's start with the happy path, where the customer should be allowed to change the delivery address… and see if it's as 'easy' as Dave thinks it will be. What would be a typical example for this?", asks Tracey.

"Yes, this is the case where the order is in preparation", starts Patricia. Tracey, who volunteered to facilitate the meeting today, takes a green card and writes *Order is in preparation* on the top of it.

"Which persona shall we use to describe this example?", asks Patricia and they all look at the wall where posters of different user types, called ***personas***[30] are displayed. The team introduced the personas a year ago when Ulla, the UX expert joined the company.

"Let's use Peter! He regularly orders pizzas at home and at the office. He probably gets the delivery address mixed up from time to time", suggests Dishita.

"OK. So let's say that Peter is in the office, but orders a Margherita pizza for home by mistake. The order has been placed and the restaurant starts to prepare it. He checks his emails a few minutes later and realizes he's used the wrong address. He clicks on the tracking link from the email and chooses 'Change Address' on the tracking page. He selects the work address and submits the changes. The change is accepted", explains Patricia.

[30] https://en.wikipedia.org/wiki/Persona_(user_experience)

"What do you mean by 'a few minutes later?'" asks Dishita.

"The order has just been received, so the pizza isn't ready yet" answers Patricia.

"Ah, OK. So the pizza might be in the oven, but it's not ready for delivery?" checks Tracey.

"Yes, that's right" replies Patricia.

While she is explaining the details, they all look at the printed UI wireframes for the new "update address" page, to help follow the example easily. Tracey captures the important steps on a green card:

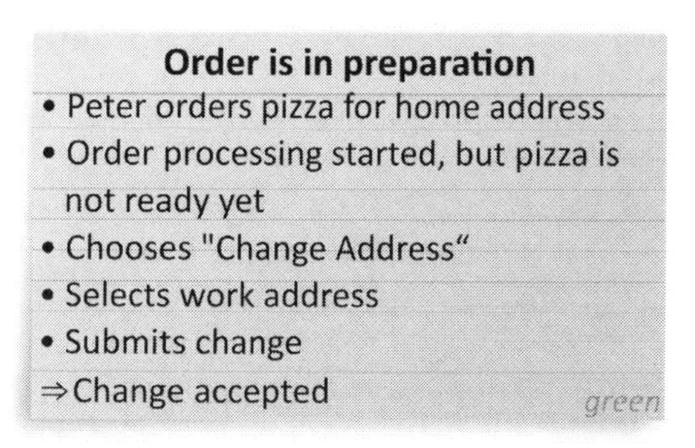

Figure 7 – The first example card

They are all following Tracey as she captures these steps, so that they can verify if the details have been captured properly.

"Is it 'not ready' or 'in preparation' that we have to watch for?", asks Ian. "We use one in the example title and the other in the second step of the example"

"Those two states mean essentially the same thing", answers Dave. "If the pizza is in preparation, then it's obviously not ready."

"We just learnt about state diagrams in our UML module at university. Is that something we could use here?" asks Ian.

Dishita grabs a pen and stands at the whiteboard. "We don't need a full UML state diagram, but I think an overview of the states would be useful, as well as some of the events." It takes a few minutes to come up with a state diagram, similar to the one below.

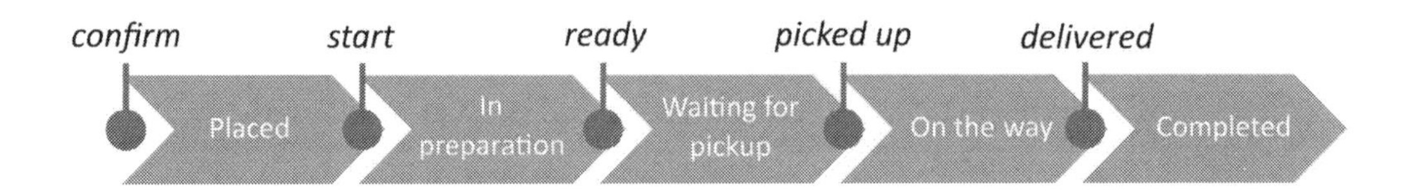

Figure 8 – State diagram of pizza process

"Then why don't we let them change the address up until the delivery person picks up the pizza?" asks Tracey. They all look at Patricia.

"That's a good point, Tracey. Actually the important turning point is when the delivery person picks up the order. This is when they check the delivery address and plan the route", concludes Patricia.

"OK. I'll fix the example card", says Tracey and changes the card to look like this:

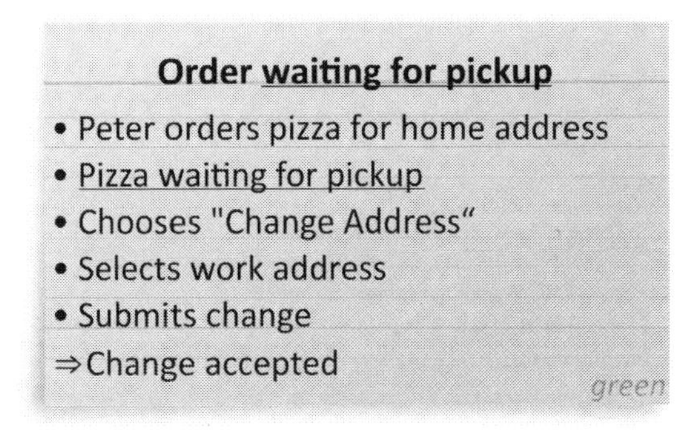

Figure 9 – The corrected example card (changes underlined)

"Is everybody happy with this?" Everyone nods, so she places the card below the story card on the desk. "What rule is this example illustrating?"

"'Allow address change if not picked up yet'", replies Patricia and she picks a blue card, writes this rule on it and places it above the green card.

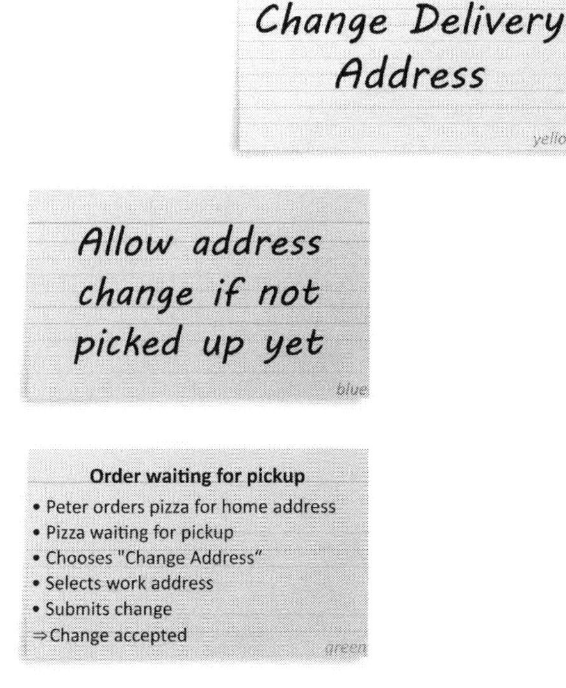

Figure 10 – First rule in the example map

"What kind of other examples can we imagine for this rule? Is there a counter-example?", Tracey helps to move the meeting forward.

"Sure! If the order has been already picked up, we should respond with a big fat error message", Dave replies promptly and smiles. "Easy..."

Everyone tries to imagine the situation... somehow it feels wrong. Dishita finally comes up with an example.

"Let's look at our other persona, Tim. He is a first time buyer, so he has to type in the delivery address. What if he makes a small mistake? I once mixed up the house number in one of my orders and only realized it when I got hungry and checked the notification mail."

"But we can't just let them change the address to a completely different location, once the pizza is already at the doorstep of the original delivery address..." says Patricia.

They start a discussion about possible options, but the discussion gets stuck. "There are lots of ways we could handle a late change of delivery address, but none of them are simple. Do we really need to do this now?" asks Dave.

"It looks like we can't solve this now. Let's make a red card for it, and check the statistics to see how often this happens and how much extra cost is caused by this sort of mistake", Tracey suggests.

They all agree, so she takes a red card and summarizes the problem. They use the red cards to track questions or other discussion points that they cannot solve immediately. They place the red cards on the desk, so that everyone can see them. This way they can avoid endless discussions about the topic.

"Can we come up with a temporary workaround for the problem?", asks Tracey once she has finished writing down the question.

"Maybe we could change the error message to advise the users to call the operator", suggests Ian.

"Very good! Let's capture that quickly before we forget!" replies Patricia and they capture another example and place it under the previous one.

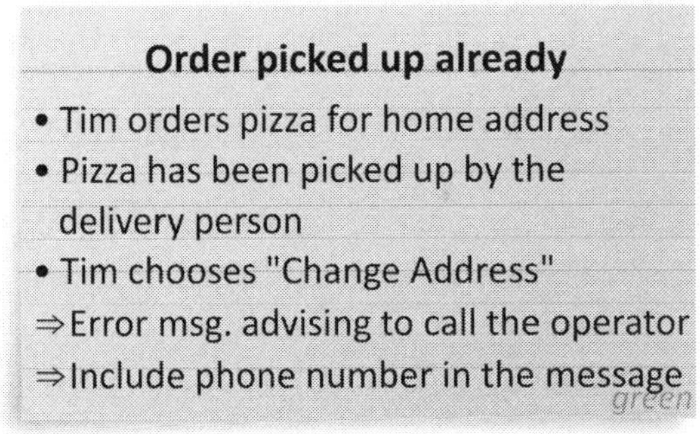

Order picked up already

- Tim orders pizza for home address
- Pizza has been picked up by the delivery person
- Tim chooses "Change Address"

⇒Error msg. advising to call the operator
⇒Include phone number in the message

green

Figure 11 – The second example card

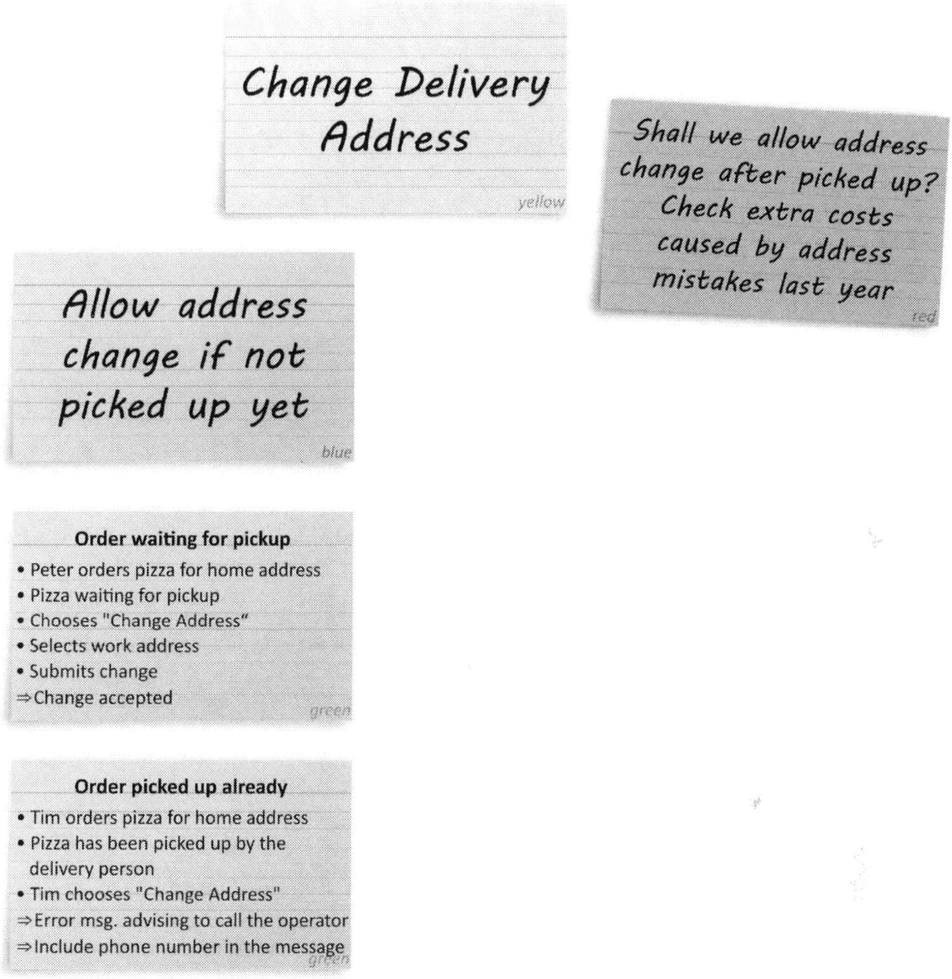

Change Delivery Address

yellow

Shall we allow address change after picked up? Check extra costs caused by address mistakes last year

red

Allow address change if not picked up yet

blue

Order waiting for pickup

- Peter orders pizza for home address
- Pizza waiting for pickup
- Chooses "Change Address"
- Selects work address
- Submits change

⇒Change accepted

green

Order picked up already

- Tim orders pizza for home address
- Pizza has been picked up by the delivery person
- Tim chooses "Change Address"

⇒Error msg. advising to call the operator
⇒Include phone number in the message

green

Figure 12 – A counter example and a question

They all look at the examples to see how the system will behave in the different situations.

"There's another one!" cries out Tracey. "What if the pizza was picked up while Tim was typing in the new address in the address change screen?"

The team realize that this illustrates the need for state verification both when the address change screen is opened and also when the change is submitted. This means that even though it's an edge case, it's important enough to capture it as a third example of the rule.

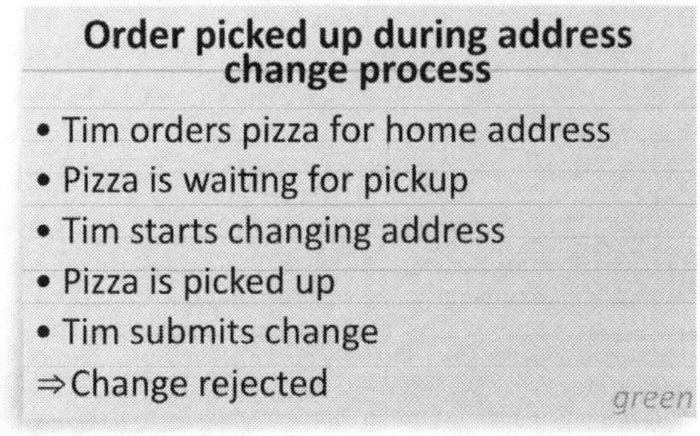

Order picked up during address change process

- Tim orders pizza for home address
- Pizza is waiting for pickup
- Tim starts changing address
- Pizza is picked up
- Tim submits change

⇒Change rejected

green

Figure 13 – The third example card

They cannot come up with any further relevant example, so they move on.

"Is this what you call 'easy', Dave?", asks Patricia.

"Well... at least we've learned a lot about the address change process", acknowledges Dave.

The team then discuss other business rules, like *only valid address is accepted, estimated time of arrival is updated* or *new address should be within restaurant's delivery range.* They come up with examples for all these rules and lay them on the desk.

The workshop finishes in about half an hour, Tracey takes a photograph of the example map (Figure 14) and everyone goes back to their desk.

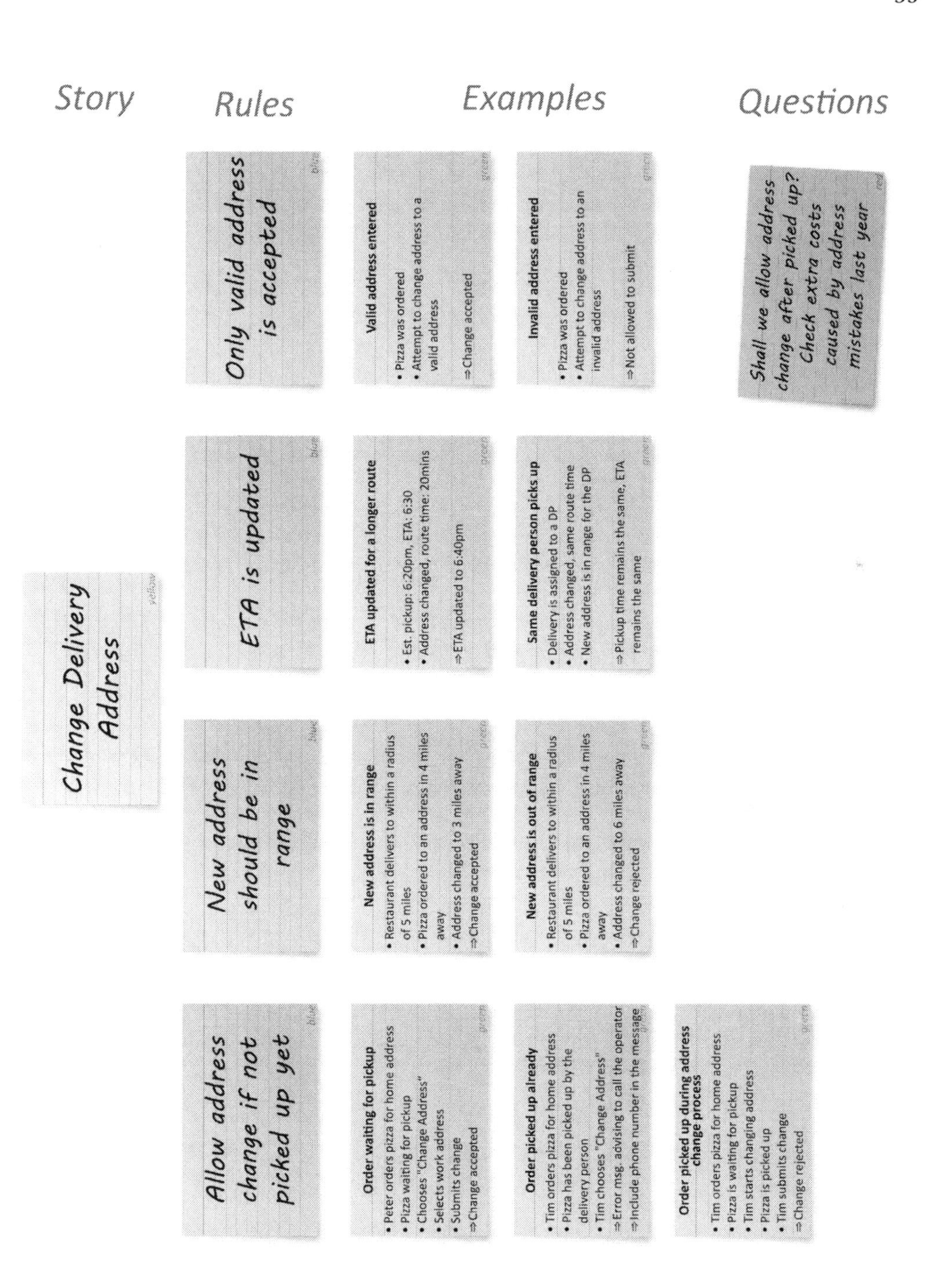

Figure 14 – The final example map

2.4 – Deliberate discovery

Developing software is a process of learning. I've never met a team that, after they deliver some working software, say "if we were to do that again, we'd do it exactly the same way." That's because, in the course of developing the software, they discover things that they didn't know at the beginning.

Discovery that happens while you're developing software can be thought of as "accidental discovery" - it may upset your schedule, or even derail or interrupt your roadmap entirely. The discovery that happens during a requirement workshop is "***deliberate discovery***." The meeting is convened with the almost-certain knowledge that there are things that we don't know. We deliberately explore our understanding of the requirements using concrete examples and, more often than not, we are rewarded by learning things. The alternative is that the learning happens, accidentally, after the delivery team has already started developing the solution.

While our team were discussing the "allow delivery address change" requirement above, examples turned out to be very useful. The rule started off looking really simple, but when they started coming up with examples to illustrate the rule, they found that they didn't have a shared understanding of the possible states of an order. They cleared this up with a state diagram, which ultimately led to them modifying the rule to "Allow address change when order not picked up."

The next example dug into what should happen when the order has been picked up, which has implications for the user experience. They came up with a simple solution and wrote out a question card to be answered by the business. This naturally led them to think about what should happen if the order is picked up *while* the address change is being requested, and they discovered another important behaviour.

Examples are used both to illustrate what we already know and to force us to question our assumptions. They underpin the deliberate discovery conversation.

2.5 – Example Mapping in a nutshell

> "Example Mapping is a simple, low-tech method for making conversations short and powerfully productive." - Matt Wynne

The ***Example Mapping*** technique[31] was discovered/invented by Matt Wynne who regularly facilitates requirement workshops for his customers. At one of his workshops, he had a pack of 4-colored index cards with him. He used the green cards to capture examples and grouped them by rules, which he wrote on blue cards. He discovered that arranging these cards as a map helps guide the discussion and gives a good visual overview of the requirements.

When participating in an Example Mapping workshop, we capture different artifacts on differently colored index cards or post-it notes.

- ***Examples*** are captured on **green cards** – illustrate concrete behaviour of the system.
- ***Rules*** are written on **blue cards** – these are logical groupings of the examples usually focusing on a particular condition. Many teams call these ***acceptance criteria*** (AC), ***business rules***, or simply ***requirements***.
- ***Questions*** or ***assumptions*** are captured on **red cards** – any topic that would block the discussion. Since these are visible to everyone, we can avoid re-discussing these (usually frustrating) topics again and again.
- ***User stories*** are captured on **yellow cards** – we usually start discussing a single user story, but as we are digging into the details, we often decide to split the story into smaller stories and postpone some of them.

Seb's story: Business rules, requirements, acceptance criteria

When my teams start discussing a user story what they typically want to understand is the scope of the story and how difficult it might be to implement. Examples really help us understand how the story is supposed to behave, but we want them in related groups.

These groupings have been called different things by different teams: business rules, acceptance criteria, requirements. Each of the terms comes with its own baggage and often hampers communication on the team. Instead, we've started just calling them *rules* - they're abstract statements that describe a single aspect

[31] https://cucumber.io/blog/2015/12/08/example-mapping-introduction

of behaviour.

An added bonus is that when it comes to splitting a story, we can often split them simply by moving some rules (and their associated examples) to a new story.

We place the story card on the top row and arrange the rules in a row underneath. The examples belonging to a particular rule are placed below the rule card they relate to. We put the red cards to the side of the example map. At the end of the discussion the desk should look like Figure 14.

Gaspar's story: Rejoining a discussion

We all have been in meetings where a notification on our phone or some other interruption distracts our focus. Once you fall out of an animated discussion, it is very hard to get back into it. These kinds of problems can be minimized by establishing a better meeting culture, but they cannot be avoided completely. So, we'd better accept that this might happen and create an infrastructure that helps the people get back into the discussion as quickly as possible. Having a visual map (or a mindmap) that is visible to everyone makes it easier to see the big picture and check the details at the same time.

The example cards will be used later when we come to write our scenarios. It does not matter what format you use to write examples as long as you capture all the details that seemed important in the discussion. For example, even if you use Cucumber, you should not use *Given/When/Then* to write your examples.

When we have captured an example, we give it a title, so that we can refer to it easily. One simple way of coming up with a title is to copy the way that episodes of the *Friends* sitcom were named: *"The One Where Rachel Finds Out"*. The words you put after the *"The One Where ..."* happen to be very good titles for our examples. *"The One Where the **Order has been Picked Up Already**"*.

There's no strict order you should collect the examples and the rules in. If the story is simple or well prepared, it will probably arrive with an initial set of rules (or acceptance criteria). In this case it makes sense to go through these rules and understand their details by creating examples that illustrate each of them.

In other situations, where the story is more vague, it might make sense to come up with some examples that describe the typical behaviours that will be expected. Then, identify the rules that govern them.

No matter how you do it, it is practical to nominate a ***facilitator***, who keeps the meeting going. The facilitator takes care that the discussion is captured on the cards and that everyone agrees with the form they have been written down. The facilitator is not a special role, anyone from the team can do it. We recommend you rotate this role across all team members.

With Example Mapping, you can discuss detailed requirements in a surprisingly short time. In many cases, the details of a user story can be discussed in 20-30 minutes. We've found this style of workshop can work for teams no matter what flavor of agile they're using, as we discuss in Chapter 4, *Who does what and when.* Because the workshops are short, we can run them several times a week.

Once the map has been created, it is important not to lose this information. Some teams take photos and share it with team members. Others pin the cards on a pinboard in the team room or save it as a mind map.

2.6 – How to establish structured conversations

Regardless of whether you use Example Mapping or another technique, structuring the conversations will help your requirement workshops be more focused and efficient. It's time to define exactly what we mean by ***structured conversation***. A structured conversation is a facilitated exchange of ideas that conforms to a predefined form. In the context of a requirement workshop, a structured conversation exhibit the following properties that we expand on below:

- **collaborative**: all attendees participate actively
- **diverse perspectives**: we need the three amigos

- **short**: we want regular workshops, so that the learning feedback loop stays fast
- **progressive focus**: we capture the progress of the workshop in real time, allowing the discussion to move forward quickly
- **consensus**: agreed concrete examples are the measure of the workshop's success

Collaborative

The conversations should include the entire team and encourage them to collaborate actively. In many agile projects the term *collaboration* means no more than inviting everyone to a planning meeting at which the product owner explains the requirements and everyone else listens. We need more bi-directional communication.

Gaspar's story: Help them participate in the discussion!

Once a member of my team asked me an important question after the meeting finished. "This is a pretty important question! Why didn't you ask the PO during the meeting?" I asked back trying to hide my emotions. "Because I wasn't sure I understood everything and I thought my question might have been answered anyway" he responded. I was pretty much frustrated about this and other similar situations and I was dreaming of a team consisting of communicative, active super-heroes asking questions frequently.

Soon afterwards, I was invited to a non-IT discussion once, where neither the topic nor the language were well known to me. I feared that I would not be able to participate properly in the discussion. The organizer helped me out by giving me a handout that contained the agenda, the discussion points and a few important sentences. Without these, I might have looked dumb, but instead I was able to participate in the discussion. Impressed by this experience I revised my attitude to team work.

Identifying the root causes of communication problems and figuring out how to

> solve them is far better than dreaming of perfection and whining when you can't achieve it. Working with an all-super-hero team must be really boring.

Everyone has a slightly different personality. You should establish a culture where everyone can participate, regardless of their personality. By using a method that requires people to stand up and move, talk to each other and arrange/annotate colored cards, we can exercise different senses, so everyone can contribute in the areas that they feel most comfortable with. For distributed teams, the possibilities are more limited, but with a few smart ideas the same efficiency can be achieved (see more on this in Chapter 4, *Who does what and when*).

Diverse perspectives

We uncover ambiguities by organizing requirement workshops where the representatives of diverse perspectives (business, test, development) come together. These meetings are sometimes called ***Three Amigos***[32] meetings. Despite the name, the point is not that there should be only three people in the room. In your team there might be other roles as well (e.g. UX) or you might invite multiple representatives of the same role. What makes these meetings powerful is that the representatives of the different roles can challenge their understanding of the requirements at an early stage. Even though they are all talking about the same requirement, each person has their own perspective:

- the business representative focuses on the fulfillment of the business goals – for example when Patricia agrees that the address can be changed before the order is picked up
- the developers explore the technical implications of the feature – for example when Dave concludes that all solutions for late change of delivery address will introduce costly complexities
- the testers can challenge the feasibility of testing the feature and help identify special corner cases – for example when Tracey noticed that the order might be picked up while the client was changing the delivery address

[32]https://www.infoq.com/interviews/george-dinwiddie-three-amigos

Short

We suggest that requirement workshops should be no longer than 30 minutes. This is a because:

- long meeting are exhausting - you'll often not get active participation from all attendees throughout the meeting
- long meetings are expensive – multiply the time by the number of people in the room and you frequently find meetings that cost a person-day
- short meetings can be scheduled more frequently – shorter meetings are less disruptive and are easier to schedule
- frequent meetings can vary the attendees – we can improve shared ownership by ensuring that it's not always the same people at the meeting
- frequent meetings reduce the impact of unanswerable questions – we can continue the discussion as soon as we discover the answer

Your situation may require longer, infrequent meetings, but even then we urge you to structure each meeting into several short, focused sessions.

Progressive focus

We start the workshop knowing what we're going to discuss, but we never know quite what we'll discover. However, as the workshop unfolds we must capture what we learn, so that at the end we have a full record of our knowledge. Our understanding becomes progressively more complete, while the record allows us to maintain focus on what we still don't understand.

Seb's story: Progressive JPEG

I think of a structured conversation as being a bit like a JPEG image downloading over a slow connection. The image becomes progressively more and more detailed. Early on you can often guess what it's an image of, but it's not until it finishes downloading that you can see the picture in its full glory.

For our conversation to keep focused while our understanding develops progressively, we need to:

- know what we're meeting about – Patricia emailed out the story for discussion the day before
- capture our understanding as it develops – the format is not important, but it must be low friction and captured continuously
- be able to quickly grasp the state of the discussion – by capturing our understanding in a form that is readable by everyone, such as an example map
- stop discussions that aren't going anywhere – for example, by capturing unanswerable questions rather than discussing them fruitlessly

Consensus

We know we have achieved consensus when we agree:

- that the output is correct – the output may not be complete, but everything in it must be agreed by everybody
- whether the feature is sufficiently understood – if it is then it needs no further discussion and development can proceed
- there is no hidden/private knowledge – the content of all conversations is captured in the output and there is no need to consolidate private notes, email chains etc.
- who is responsible for answering each remaining question – capturing questions is a great way to keep the discussion moving, but someone needs to ensure that they get answered

2.7 – What we just learned

Software development is a learning process. The more we can learn about the problem, the easier solving it becomes. This process can be made more effective by having several team members (with different perspectives) analyzing the requirements together *before they start developing the software.* These collaborative requirement workshops are most productive if they are kept short and run regularly throughout the project – often several times a week.

There are many structured conversation techniques that have been used to facilitate these requirement workshops, but the most useful that we have come across is Example Mapping, as described by Matt Wynne. It's simple, well documented and results in a visual recording of the conversation that clearly communicates the agreements that were reached, as well as the questions that remain unanswered. This in turn makes it easier for those that weren't at the meeting to understand the issues and provide useful feedback.

All software development projects depend on well understood requirements, but the approach described here works particularly well for the lightweight agile and lean methods that are in common use today.

Chapter 3 – What is an example?

In the previous chapters, we explored the role of examples in a BDD approach. You may have wondered: "Are examples really enough to specify a feature? How many examples do we need to specify a feature?"

In this chapter, we're going to answer these questions.

3.1 – How hard is concrete?

We all know what an example is, but when it comes to creating concrete examples that unambiguously illustrate how a system should behave, we need to ensure they're good examples. It's best to think of an example as being an artifact divided into 3 parts - context, action and outcome - and to think of these in the *opposite* order.

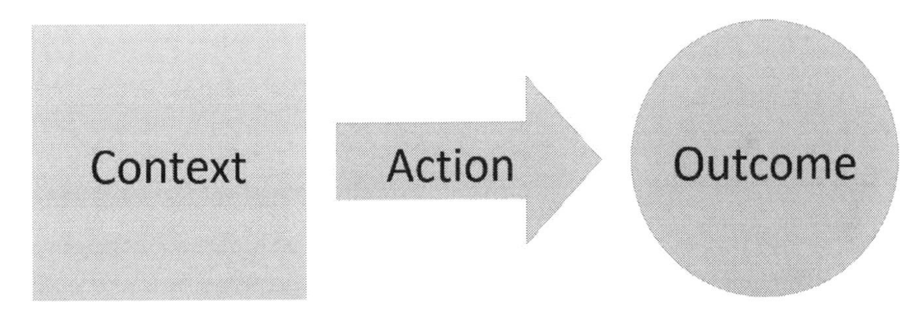

Figure 15 – Anatomy of an example

The *outcome* is a description of the state of the system after the behaviour we're interested in has taken place. It should contain enough detail so that we could actually go and check that the system has behaved according to our expectations.

The *action* is the event that causes the behaviour we're interested in to take place. It might be some action by a user, but equally it might be an input from another system, a scheduled job, or any other stimulus that can cause the system to react.

The *context* describes the state the system is in *before* the action takes place. Sometimes, when the starting context is *obvious*, it can be tempting to omit describing the context. Don't do this! Once you are very familiar with creating concrete examples you might consider revisiting this advice, but not yet.

Seb's story: Illustrating things with concrete

I often find myself explaining why we use the word 'concrete' when talking about examples. Rules are generic expressions of how the system ought to behave – they each cover lots of possible situations. An example, on the other hand, expresses a single situation that illustrates an interesting application of a rule. This expression should leave no room for ambiguity – it's whole purpose is to clarify a rule – so we need to be specific and precise.

The term 'concrete' is often used to mean that we are dealing with specific details, and that is the context that we are using it in when we talk about 'concrete examples'.

When specifying a concrete example, the context, action and outcome all need to specify concrete data. Imagine you had to actually run through the example using the real system - what data would need to be provided for you to cause the system to verifiably behave in the expected way? Use actual text strings and values - usernames, passwords, amounts of money, dates of transactions.

3.2 – Is all that concrete essential?

Most systems are complex enough to need large amounts of context data (e.g. reference data tables, user accounts, inventories) before they can exhibit the behaviours we're interested in. Does that mean every example has to specify all this information? That would make for very long, boring examples, so thankfully the answer is "NO!"

Each example illustrates a single rule, and should only mention concrete data that is directly related to the behaviour being illustrated. Imagine you're writing examples that illustrate changing the delivery address after a customer places an order for a pizza. Does the example's context need to specify the type of pizza being ordered?

Or that the customer's payment was successfully authorized? No. There will be other rules that govern having pizza choice and successful payment. These will be illustrated by examples that focus on the essential, concrete data that relates to those behaviours. The example that illustrates changing a delivery address should only contain enough information to determine that the address change is processed correctly - nothing more.

Remember that the purpose of the requirement workshop is to use concrete examples to quickly explore the requirement and demonstrate that everyone understands exactly what is being asked for. Getting the right level of detail is not our primary concern - inessential detail will be removed later when we formulate the example as a scenario (see *The BDD Books: Formulation*[33]).

3.3 – How many examples do we need?

Let's have a look at the rule that our team discussed in Chapter 2, *Structured conversation.*

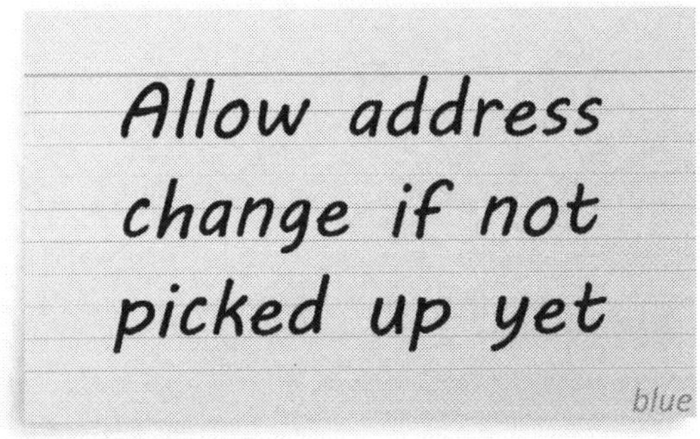

Figure 16 – Address change rule

The team were exploring the address change functionality and came to the conclusion that the address can only be changed before an order is picked up by a delivery person. This means that the delivery address can't be changed once an order has progressed beyond the *waiting for pickup* state.

[33]Nagy, Gáspár, and Seb Rose. *The BDD Books: Formulation.* In preparation. http://bddbooks.com/formulation.

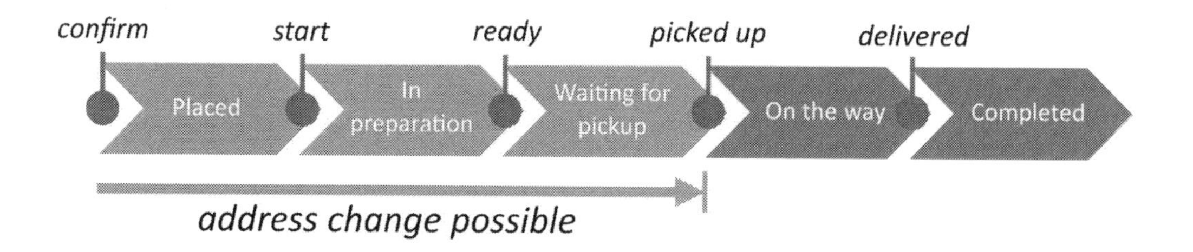

Figure 17 – Order states

You probably remember that there was a misunderstanding between team members during the discussion. Initially, the rule stated that the address could be changed *before* an order is *waiting for pickup* (which means it has not progressed beyond the *in preparation* state). The team resolved the misunderstanding using concrete examples, but it could still be implemented incorrectly!

Without knowing much about the application, we can imagine that this functionality will be implemented using an `if` statement, that will look something like this:

```
if (order.State <= OrderState.WaitingForPickup)
    ...
```

So, let's imagine that Dave, who developed this feature, uses < instead of <= in this condition. This is the sort of mistake that is easy to make, even though the developer is fully aware of the requirement details.

The team described two examples for the rule:

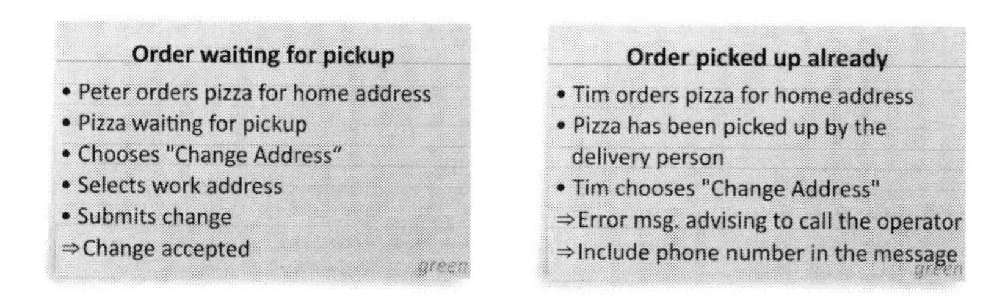

Figure 18 – Examples for the address change rule

In the first example, the phrase "Pizza prepared and waiting for pickup" refers exactly to the *waiting for pickup* state. This is good news, because if Dave misses the = from the condition, the first example will not be satisfied.

Does this mean that these two examples are *enough*? Will they catch all possible programming mistakes? Certainly not.

Shall we add more examples then? Shall we capture examples for all possible states?

3.4 – Why stop now?

Catching all implementation mistakes will be important, but during the discovery phase our focus is on the requirements: *we would like to prevent bugs from ever happening*. We want to achieve this by ensuring a better understanding of the requirements. The examples that we generate during the requirement workshop illustrate the desired behaviour of the system. They demonstrate that the development team understand what they are being asked to do *and* that the business understands the implications of what they are asking for.

Once captured, examples make excellent test cases for use once the software has been developed, because they specify the *concrete* state of the system before a specific behaviour is exercised, as well as the expected outcome that should be observed.

When we start considering the exhaustive exploration of all possible combinations, we have moved away from understanding the requirements into the realm of software testing. When the examples start to address concerns that the product owner is not interested in, it's time for the facilitator to bring the discussion back on track.

This doesn't mean that we should forget about attaining "good coverage" in our tests (e.g. using the ***Classification Tree Method***[34] and ***equivalence classes***[35]), but this should be done by the delivery team outside the requirement workshop (see more on this in Chapter 4, *Who does what and when*). This will keep the conversation engaging for the product owner and the rest of the team.

[34]https://en.wikipedia.org/wiki/Classification_Tree_Method

[35]https://en.wikipedia.org/wiki/Equivalence_partitioning

3.5 – Rules vs. examples

We have discussed how examples are needed to explore and illustrate each rule (requirement, business rule, acceptance criteria). We showed that rules on their own were insufficient. Let's turn the question around: are examples alone sufficient to specify the functionality of an application?

Let's look at the examples in Figure 18 again. How easy would it be to deduce the rule (Figure 16) that they are illustrating if all you had were the examples?

Generally, we can say: it is not always possible to "reverse engineer" the rules from the examples, and it would certainly be easier if we never have to try to. Examples *illustrate* the rules, but they do not replace them. Whenever we capture examples, we have to make sure that we also record the rule as well, because both are needed to document the expected behaviour of the system. The rules provide the concise, abstract description, and the examples provide precise, concrete illustrations of them.

This is nothing new - it's how we learn anyway. When parents want to teach their young child the danger of fire, they explain that it hurts and say ("Never put your finger into a fire"). This is the rule. To illustrate this, they might put their own finger over a candle flame (smarter parents only pretend) and cry out to show that it was painful. This is the example.

Why "Specification by Example"?

You might have seen the term ***Specification by Example*** and assumed that this meant examples were sufficient to specify software. The intent, however, is to emphasize the *use* of examples to support a specification by making it harder for the rules to be misinterpreted.

The product owner usually wants the delivery team to solve some specific problem. She will often come to the team with a high level user story and some acceptance criteria, but where did they come from?

The usual way we start thinking about any problem is to think about some situations in which it occurs (e.g. examples). Once a good enough understanding of the general problem has been understood, we'll then try to express this as business rules or acceptance criteria. This is the process that product owners (and business analysts) frequently go through before they talk to the team. Then, in the requirement workshop, the team explores their understanding by coming up with more examples which test that the rules have been expressed correctly. Finally, the development team will write some software, and it's the rule that gets implemented, while the examples make great test cases.

We need to document the rules even when, later, we formulate the examples into scenarios. More on this in *The BDD Books: Formulation*[36].

While rules and examples are extremely powerful ways to specify the behaviour of software, there are other tools that complement them. Definitions, model diagrams, formulas, glossaries and other artifacts might also be necessary as part of the specification.

3.6 – My example illustrates multiple rules!

During the requirement workshops, we break down the user stories into rules (or acceptance criteria) and then we illustrate these rules with examples. When using ***Example Mapping***, we would like to produce a tidy map with a collection of examples underneath each rule, something like the one shown in Figure 14. Sometimes this can be tricky. Depending on the situation, you might find an example that illustrates multiple rules at once. Is this a problem?

As we discussed in Chapter 2, *Structured conversation*, we use rules and examples to structure our conversations, to make our requirement workshops more efficient. To be able to focus on a particular aspect of the problem, we should try to come up with examples that are focused, ie. they illustrate only one rule.

Focusing on a rule and utilizing it are two different things though. Looking back at our example, we can see that we have multiple rules that are related to the address change. For example, we have a rule that only a valid address is accepted. We also have a rule that you can change the address only if the order has not been picked up yet. Let's have a look at the positive example of the second rule:

[36]Nagy, Gáspár, and Seb Rose. *The BDD Books: Formulation*. In preparation. http://bddbooks.com/formulation.

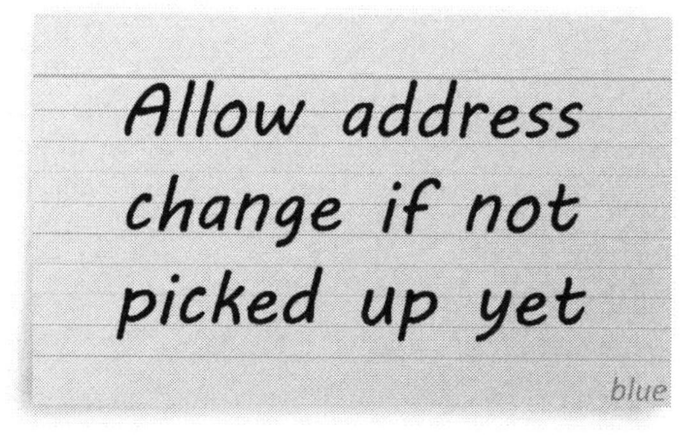

Order waiting for pickup

- Peter orders pizza for home address
- Pizza waiting for pickup
- Chooses "Change Address"
- Selects work address
- Submits change

⇒Change accepted

green

Figure 19 – Positive example of the order state rule

As you can see, this example describes a successful address change and this implies that all other rules – including the valid address rule – have to be satisfied. So, we had to pick a valid address.

Let's take a closer look at this example. Does it *utilize* the valid address rule? Yes, it does! Does it *focus* on address validity? No, it doesn't! Does it *illustrate* the valid address rule? This is more difficult to answer, because this concrete example would probably work as a positive example even for the address validity rule. Still, the way the example has been written directs the attention to the order state and not to the validity of the address. Let's contrast it with the positive example of the valid address rule:

Figure 20 – Positive example of the valid address rule

As you can see, the final result is the same ("Change accepted"), but the phrasing of the example helps us to focus on the address validity.

If you find yourself writing a single example that illustrates multiple rules, don't worry. Before you finish the workshop, consider splitting the example up into several examples that each focus on a single rule. When you do this, you'll probably find that some of the concrete data essential to illustrate one of the rules is not essential to illustrate the other(s).

3.7 – The bigger picture

Short focused examples are great to illustrate the behaviour of a single rule, but don't give you a good overview of a whole interaction with the system. Other forms of documentation are useful to get a feel for how the system will behave. We often use wireframes, page-flows, and box-and-arrow diagrams of all varieties.

Remember, the Agile Manifesto asks us to value working software over comprehensive documentation, not to dispense with documentation entirely.

3.8 - What we just learned

The requirement workshop is an excellent place to challenge the teams' understanding of the requirements. In this chapter we have seen that it can take quite a bit of practice to get good at creating the concrete examples that drive away ambiguity, while keeping them easy to read and maintain. Nor are examples on their own sufficient – they need to be created to illustrate business rules, and those rules should be documented alongside the examples.

We discussed the anatomy of a good example, made up of context, action and outcome, and emphasized the need to use appropriate *concrete* data. And we've warned you that an example should usually illustrate a single rule and contain only data that is essential to understand the behaviour of that rule. We've mentioned that other forms of documentation are needed to paint the bigger picture.

Getting good takes time, but getting started is a simple matter of giving it a try. You now have enough information to make a good start. In the next chapter we'll talk more about who does what (and when) in the BDD approach.

Chapter 4 – Who does what and when

In the previous chapters, we discussed the importance of collaboration for a BDD approach to be successful. In this chapter, we will show how BDD can be integrated into the development process and answer some common questions, like "Who should write the scenarios?", "Who do we need to participate in the requirement workshops?", and "Should the testers or the developers automate the scenarios?".

In this chapter we're going to describe the BDD approach in more detail. We'll also provide some examples of how BDD has been successfully adopted by various organizations using different development processes. Don't treat these as best practice checklists, but rather as starting points that allow you to develop a process that fits your project.

Remember that every project is different. They follow different development processes (such as Scrum or Kanban). They are integrated into a company culture that has its own definition of what each role is responsible for. For example, how much development skill should a *tester* have? Individual team members will have different backgrounds and personalities.

The most successful projects consider all these factors when defining their development process (and understand that this process has to be reviewed and adapted as necessary).

4.1 – The BDD approach

To be able to discuss how to integrate BDD into your development process, let's look at the BDD approach in more detail and let's list the different tasks or activities that are typically involved.

You probably remember from the high level overview of the BDD approach that we provided in Chapter 1, *What is BDD?*:

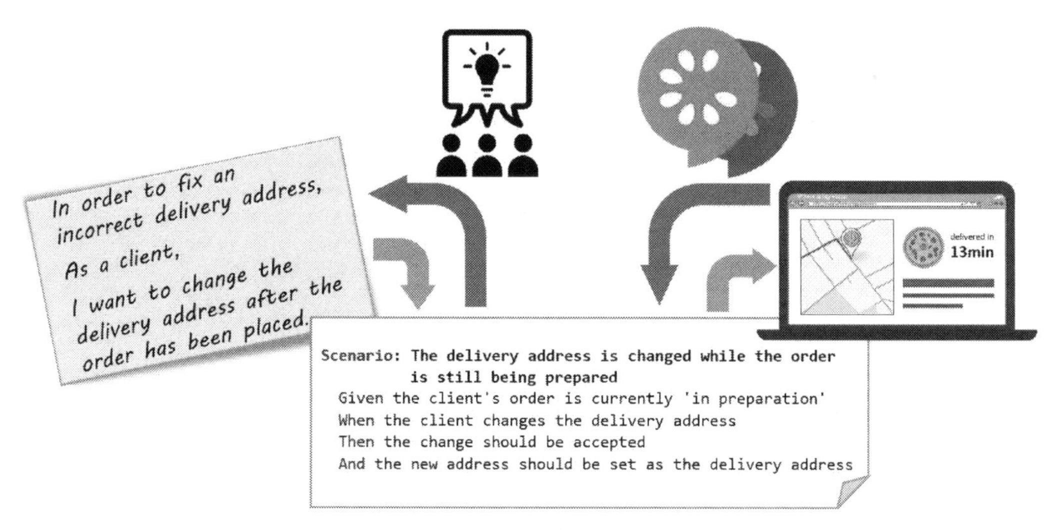

Figure 21 – High level BDD approach

In practice, the BDD approach is more complex and consists of several connected activities, which we will discuss in detail. To get started, take a look at the following diagram (Figure 22):

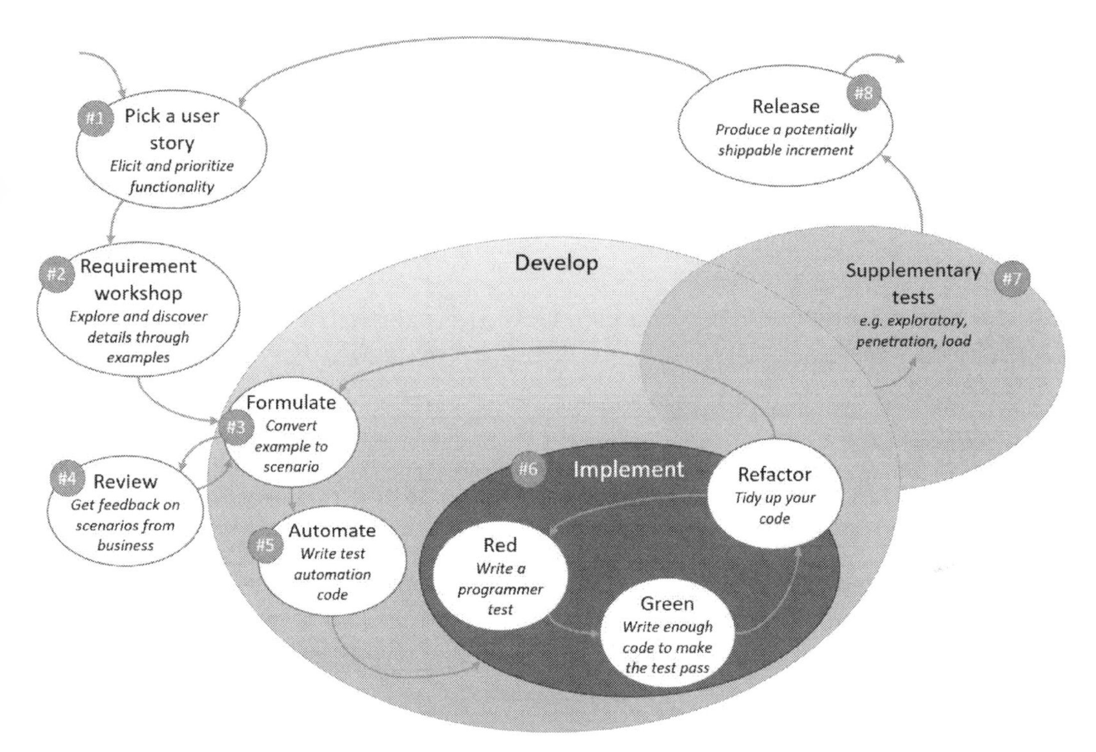

Figure 22 – Tasks and activities in the BDD approach

The following list contains a brief overview of these tasks. In the list we describe the ideal timing, the team members involved and also the expected outcome.

#1 – Pick a user story

What: Requirements elicitation and prioritization.

When: Before the requirement workshop – preferably at least a day in advance.

Who: Product owner, business analyst, customer, key stakeholders

Outcome: A candidate user story, scoped with relevant business rules (acceptance criteria). There should be enough detail to allow the development team to explore the scope of the story using concrete examples.

#2 – Requirement workshop

What: Discuss the user story by focusing on rules and examples.

When: Regularly throughout the project – we recommend running short workshops several times a week.

Who: All roles must be represented at this meeting (at least the three amigos), but multiple representatives of each role can attend. As we described in Section 2.6, *How to establish structured conversations*, each role representative has their own responsibility and focus.

Outcome: The candidate story is refined, and is frequently decomposed into smaller stories, each accompanied by a set of rules and examples. The examples should be captured in as light a format as possible, and should not be written using *Given/When/Then.*

#3 – Formulate

What: Formulate the examples into scenarios.

When: Before the implementation of the story starts. Best done as the first task of development, but sometimes done as a separate workshop where all scenarios scheduled for the iteration are formulated.

Who: In the beginning, when the language and style we use to phrase the scenarios is still being established, it is recommended to do it with the entire team. Later, it can be efficiently done by a pair: a developer (or someone who is responsible for the automation) and a tester (or someone who is responsible for quality) as long as their output is actively reviewed by a business representative.

Outcome: Scenarios added to source control. The language of the scenarios is business readable and consistent.

#4 – Review

What: Review the scenarios to ensure they correctly describe expected business behaviour.

When: Whenever a scenario is written or modified.

Who: Product owner (and maybe business analyst, customer, key stakeholders).

Outcome: Confidence that the development team have correctly understood the requirements of the business; the behaviour is expressed using appropriate terminology.

Seb's story: Hand gun in the carry-on luggage

I was going through security at the airport and the security guard called me over after my carry-on luggage had been X-rayed. "Sir", he said "there appears to be a hand gun in your luggage". I was very surprised. I don't usually travel with a hand gun!

It turns out that watching X-rays of other people's luggage is not the world's most interesting job. To keep the security guards alert, the software randomly superimposes the image of a forbidden item on the X-ray.

Reviewing scenarios is an important job, and it's the job of those that write the scenarios to make sure that they are interesting enough to keep their business colleagues eager to review them. It's all too easy to write verbose, repetitive scenarios that are difficult and boring to read. When this happens, you might just get a short review response, such as "Looks fine to me".

To check that the scenarios really are interesting enough to read, occasionally leave one out (or add an incorrect one). If you don't get feedback on your deliberate mistake it probably means that you need to work with your business to understand what level of detail they are interested in having documented.

#5 – Automate

What: Automate the scenarios by writing test automation code.

When: Automate scenarios before starting the implementation, following a test-driven approach. This way the implementation can be "driven" by the scenarios, so the application will be designed for testability and the development team will have greater focus on real outcomes.

Some teams do the automation task separately or even (especially when the application is only automated through the UI) after the implementation is finished. This approach reduces the advantages of BDD, but the end result might be still better than doing ad-hoc integration testing or no testing at all. You may find yourself working in this way as a part of a cultural change, but try to not get stuck here.

Who: Developers or test automation experts. When doing pair programming, pairing a developer with a tester works well.

Whether scenarios should be automated by developers or testers is very dependent on the company culture and the team setup. It is definitely true that for some complex, design-related aspects of the test automation infrastructure, developers are necessary. On the other hand, a good automation infrastructure may enable team members, with less coding experience, to perform automation tasks.

Outcome: Set of (failing) automated scenarios that can be executed both locally and in continuous integration/delivery/deployment environments.

#6 – Implement

What: Implement the application code to make the automated scenarios pass. We show this as the classic TDD cycle of Red/Green/Refactor, with programmer tests driving the implementation.

When: Implementation starts as soon as the first scenario has been automated, so the implementation is being driven by a failing scenario.

Who: Developers.

Outcome: A working application that behaves as specified. This can be verified automatically.

#7 – Supplementary test

What: Perform manual and other forms of testing, described in your testing strategy. This can include scripted, manual testing, exploratory testing, performance, security or other testing. For more details see quadrants 3 and 4 in the Agile Testing Quadrants[37].

[37] http://lisacrispin.com/2011/11/08/using-the-agile-testing-quadrants/

When: You don't have to wait until an entire story is finished. Scenarios provide a functional breakdown of the user story, so each scenario itself contributes a meaningful part of the application's behaviour. Therefore, as soon as there is a completed scenario, testing activities can start. (Test preparation can start even earlier, of course.)

Who: Testers – other team members can help with some aspects of testing, but these activities are usually coordinated by testers.

Outcome: High quality working application; the story is *done*.

#8 - Release

What: Produce a potentially shippable increment. This is the end of our cycle, but a released product should be used to gather feedback from the users, which can provide input to future development cycles – although this is out of scope for this book.

When: At any time that all tests are passing, but especially at the end of an iteration.

Who: The development team will be responsible for producing the releasable artifacts, but there may be specialized teams that create the actual release package.

Outcome: An installable release package.

4.2 - BDD in Scrum

Now let's take a look at a few examples of BDD being integrated into different development process models. We'll start with the most commonly used agile methodology, the Scrum framework. BDD works very well with Scrum, although many people seem to be surprised by this.

In Scrum, work is organized into sprints that are 2-4 week iterations. There are regular workshops that focus on the customer's requirements throughout each sprint (backlog refinement, backlog grooming,[38] sprint planning preparation, sprint planning) where user stories are prepared. At the sprint planning meeting, the team chooses a few stories to implement in the upcoming sprint. Once the sprint is done, the team presents their results in a sprint review/demo and potential process improvements are discussed in the sprint retrospective.

[38]Scrum no longer uses the term 'grooming', replacing it with the word 'refinement.'

Requirement workshops

Since a sprint is relatively short, and the number of stories the team usually has to deliver is small, the team can have a good overview and understanding of all the stories in the sprint backlog.

In Scrum, there are regular meetings that focus on the customer's requirements throughout each sprint, where user stories are prepared (backlog refinement and sprint planning preparation). This culminates at the sprint planning meeting, where the team finally commits to the details. When doing BDD, we explore and discover details of stories at these meetings. This can be achieved with the help of structured conversations (Chapter 2, *Structured conversation*) and an appropriate technique, such as Example Mapping (Section 2.5, *Example Mapping in a nutshell*).

If the team has good access to the product owner, we recommended that you organize short Example Mapping sessions regularly, and have these replace backlog refinement meetings. You can hold them weekly, but you might consider scheduling them several times a week, or even daily. This enables a product owner to get feedback fast from the team regarding a new idea, and removes the need for informal communication (such as e-mail threads and water-cooler conversations), where any decisions made can easily be lost or forgotten. Short, daily meetings have a lot of advantages and you can always cancel a session when your team has prepared enough stories for the next sprint.

Examples help us focus on the outcomes, even during early discussions, which improves the effectiveness of communication. If you use Example Mapping, you will spend less time on unstructured discussions, jumping between topics and re-discussing questions that cannot be answered at the meeting. Of course Example Mapping does not make complex problems simple, but your time in the session is spent on valuable discussions.

Gaspar's story: BDD works even when access to your product owner is limited

I worked on a complex legacy project, where we were committed to capturing scenarios for all new features. The customer was an agile IT company and they

> had lots of experience with Scrum.
>
> The domain was new to us and access to the product owner was limited. We were prepared for long and exhausting sprint planning meetings, but surprisingly, we were able to finish these meetings early, sprint after sprint.
>
> After one of these meetings, the product owner turned to me and asked: "How do you manage to complete the spring planning meeting so quickly? Other ones that I've been to are much longer and never finish on time."
>
> I could not really answer him at the time, because we were not intentionally doing anything special. (This was years before Example Mapping.) However, after analyzing our meetings, we realized that our commitment to writing scenarios made us focus on examples during the discussion. We did this to make it easier to formulate scenarios later, but a side-effect was that our meetings were more structured and achieved their goal more quickly.

If the access to the product owner is limited, like in Gaspar's story, you can still integrate the structured conversations and Example Mapping into the sprint planning meeting.

Formulate

Formulating an example as a scenario is tricky. It involves decisions about which word to use, how to construct a phrase and which verb tense to use. This can take a long time.

Establishing a shared understanding is important, but making the entire team discuss the best way to express a scenario in business language is not efficient. So generally, we would not recommend formulating scenarios during the preparation or planning meetings.

In Scrum, the best approach to formulating scenarios is to include it as a task in the story's implementation pipeline. This means that the first task on the taskboard for a story should be the following: formulate the examples of the story as scenarios and add them to source control. If the story is related to an area of the application where the team has no automation experience, you should consider only formulating a few representative examples into scenarios, so that you can check that their phrasing is convenient for automation. While automating these scenarios, you will learn more about the solution design and you can incorporate this knowledge into the formulation of the remaining scenarios.

Formulation is usually undertaken by a pair, often a developer and a tester. This makes it simpler to fit formulation into the sprint schedule, limits its cost and the subsequent review by the product owner ensures that the delivery team members really have understood what the business is asking of them.

We have seen teams doing formulation as a special workshop right after sprint planning (e.g. on the day following the sprint planning day), where the entire team split into smaller working groups, work on the formulation of the examples of all stories. Once the smaller groups have finished their work, the team discusses the results together. Although such workshops might be useful in the initial phase, when you learn about BDD and the domain language, it might put quite a significant administrative overhead on the team (yet another fixed day where everyone is expected to be present).

In some projects, the scenarios have to be formally approved by the product owner or someone else. In these cases, the formulation has to be prioritized and planned in a way that the team does not get blocked.

How scenarios help with the decomposition into tasks

In Scrum, stories are usually broken down into tasks. Tasks are work units that represent the design decisions of the team and they are also used to track the daily progress of the team.

The tasks are owned by the development team. The team can list anything as a task that needs to be completed to be able to finish the story. The tasks are often very technical (e.g. create a `Users` table) and do not have to be understandable by the Product Owner.

Examples and scenarios are the opposite – they describe a functional breakdown of the story and they are business-readable. Because of this, it initially seems like BDD has nothing to do with Scrum tasks and task planning. The reality is somewhat different, though. Once you have illustrated the story with a couple of key examples, the task planning becomes easier. The key examples paint the big picture and reveal the design decisions that need to be made.

Tasks are usually technical, but where practical you should try to create them so that each one relates to a single example (scenario) e.g. "Create tables for capturing the delivery address" instead of a generic "Create tables" task. This is not possible for all tasks – there might be some tasks on which several scenarios depend.

By aligning tasks to scenarios, the development team will realize several benefits:

- The team will focus on the expected behaviour during the implementation. This can help avoid "gold-plating" or implementing infrastructures that are not needed. Starting from the scenario helps follow an outside-in[39] development approach.
- You can get feedback about the story implementation earlier. Imagine you have a half-done story, where all the database tables are created, but nothing is visible for the users. Now compare it with a half-done story, where 3 of the 7 scenarios are already implemented end-to-end. The latter can be shown to the product owner to get feedback on what has been implemented so far.
- Manual testing can be started before the story is fully implemented. The execution report of the story scenarios will show which functional parts of the story are ready for testing, so testers do not require status reports to be created.
- The functional progress provides better transparency and hence increases the trust between the development team and the product owner. A progress status of 57% means nothing, but demonstrating that 3 scenarios out of 7 are already working is an achievement that can be easily understood.

For stories that involve only simple design decisions, task planning is more about having a checklist so that nothing is forgotten. For these stories, scenarios can also be used directly as tasks. e.g. "Automate & implement scenario: Delivery address is captured".

Some teams might even skip creating tasks – if the company process rules allow this. When the stories are small enough (and nicely decomposed into rules and examples) making an additional taskboard might not provide further benefits.

[39]https://en.wikipedia.org/wiki/Outside%E2%80%93in_software_development

Gaspar's story: Scenarios in the sprint review

I was working on a project where the customer was not involved directly in the BDD process, or at least she was not aware of it. She knew about Scrum and regularly participated in the Sprint reviews.

Our review was more or less typical: we went through the stories we had done and demonstrated the new features of the application. The only thing we did differently was that before starting the demonstration of a story we showed the related scenarios and read them out loud. This acted as an introduction for the upcoming demo.

After a few sprints, I intentionally "forgot" to show her the scenarios before the demo and waited to see her reaction. I got what I wanted to hear: she was missing those "nice summaries" that helped her remember the details and give better feedback.

Later, we started to use examples and scenarios in the requirement workshops as well, where they helped clear up misunderstandings before the story ever made it onto a sprint backlog.

4.3 – BDD in Lean/Kanban

Kanban[40] and other lean approaches to managing software projects are also popular nowadays, especially with development teams that are responsible for operations. Kanban optimizes end-to-end delivery ("lead time") by visualizing the workflow and limiting work in progress (WIP) to be able to detect and fix bottlenecks more easily.

[40] https://en.wikipedia.org/wiki/Kanban

If you are already familiar with Scrum and you would like to learn more about Kanban, we can recommend the mini book by Henrik Kniberg & Mattias Skarin "Kanban and Scrum - Making the Most of Both" [41]. The ebook version is available for free.

The discussion and implementation activities of the BDD approach are scoped to user stories, which are the typical work unit tracked on Kanban boards. Short, regular or ad-hoc Example Mapping sessions can be used to feed the input queues of the development team whenever the capacity (the WIP limit) allows.

If the scenario automation process requires special skills or expertise, you can visualize this on the Kanban board as a separate column, if this helps to optimize the flow (e.g. if UI automation becomes a bottleneck). Be careful with this though, because more separation of *automation* and *implementation* might reduce the positive impact of the test-driven approach we follow with BDD.

Each user story is an independent work unit, but the scenarios that illustrate its behaviour can be implemented individually. BDD tasks and activities are related to the scenarios – not the story.

Actually, the tasks *formulate*, *automate*, *implement*, *review* and *supplementary test* can be seen as a sub-workflow. This can, in principle, be visualized on the Kanban board. Keep in mind that *less is more* and make sure that this kind of tracking actually provides some benefit for your development process.

4.4 – BDD in Distributed Teams

Having a distributed team is common nowadays. In these projects the physical distance is typically combined with time zone differences, cultural distance and language barriers, as well.

However, BDD in distributed teams is carried out in the same way as for colocated teams. There are the additional communication challenges faced by all distributed teams, but the concrete examples produced during the requirement workshop can

[41]Kniberg, Henrik, Mattias Skarin, Mary Poppendieck, and David Anderson. *Kanban and Scrum: Making the Most of Both*. United States: InfoQ, 2010. Print/Web. https://www.infoq.com/minibooks/kanban-scrum-minibook.

reduce this by providing a tangible representation of the agreed behaviour of the system. Good audio-visual facilities and collaborative online tools are essential.

Providing information about the scenario implementation status (e.g. with an execution report updated as part of the CI build), can lead to improved cooperation between developers, testers, and product owners. Testers and product owners can get information directly from the scenario execution reports when they need to see if manual testing needs to be performed or if they need to make a progress report. They don't have to wait until everyone provides status information.

Requirement workshops with distributed team

The real challenge with distributed teams is finding some way to run the requirement workshops effectively, without losing the benefits of collaboration.

Example Mapping, which we have described in Section 2.5, *Example Mapping in a nutshell* uses index cards and direct communication to discover the requirement details, so some modifications will be needed for remote meetings. Let's remind ourselves of the most important characteristics of Example Mapping before considering how we might facilitate a ***remote requirement workshop***:

- focus on rules and examples when discussing the story
- nominate a facilitator who keeps the meeting going
- collect results in a format that all team members can understand, so that they can challenge them if necessary
- capture questions that block the discussion and make them visible to everyone
- provide an easy way to have an overview of what we have discussed already
- produce shared notes

The challenge is to find a way that works for your team that still delivers these characteristics. At the time of writing this book, we are not aware of any online Example Mapping tool, but it is likely that such tools will be available soon.

Currently the best result can be achieved by using Google Sheets that you share on the screens / projectors at all locations. The Figure 23 shows the same example map we showed in Chapter 2, *Structured conversation* (Figure 14) using **Google Sheets** (download template here[42]). Alternatively you can use a mind mapping tool as shown

[42]http://speclink.me/examplemaptemplate

in Figure 24, created using **MindMup 2**[43].

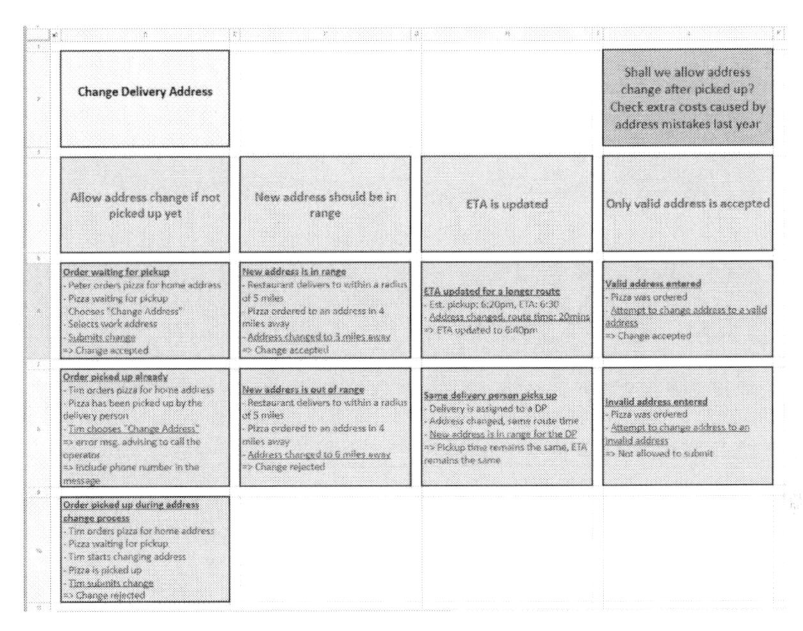

Figure 23 – Example map in Google Sheets

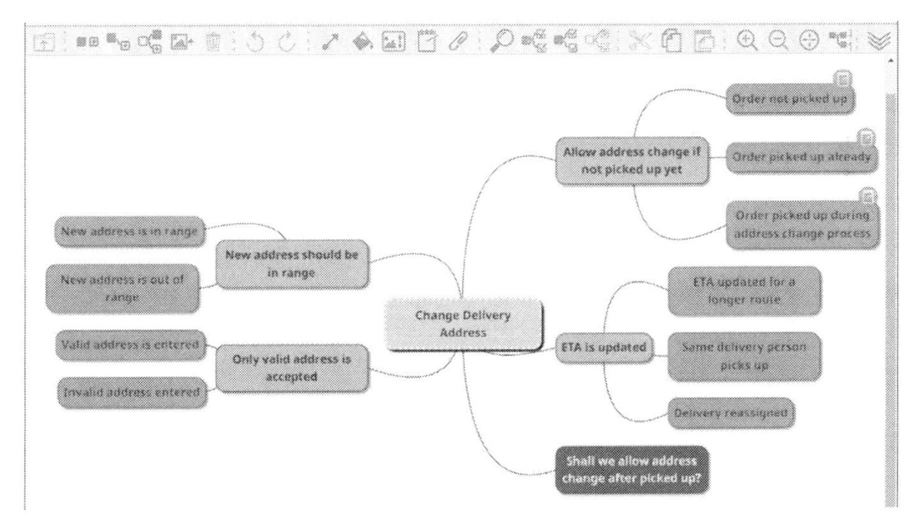

Figure 24 – Example map in mind map form

[43]https://www.mindmup.com/

For simpler stories, you can also use any note-taking application and share it on all screens. If the application supports this, you can collapse different detail levels, so that you can still have an overview of what you have discussed so far. The Figure 25 shows such an example with **Microsoft OneNote**[44].

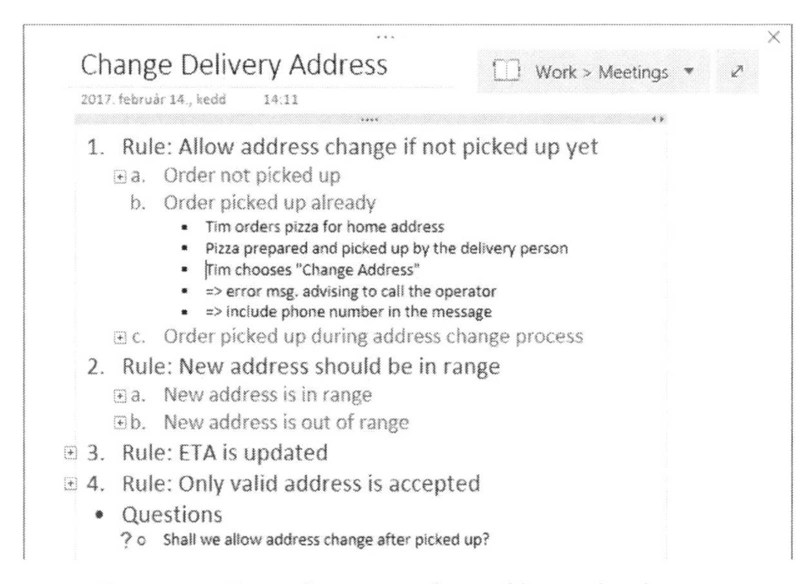

Figure 25 – Example map in a form of hierarchical notes

4.5 – BDD in fixed scope projects

Projects with fixed price, fixed scope, fixed "everything" are definitely not ideal for agile software development, especially when we're building highly complex, sophisticated and usable applications in a rapidly changing business environment. These applications typically have to integrate other external services and use disparate technologies. In this sort of environment, pretending that we can commit to scope, price and time is an illusion.

Despite this, there are many examples of projects that have to operate under these constraints. Reasons include a slowly changing company culture or over-rigid project tendering rules.

[44]https://www.onenote.com/

Can BDD be integrated into such project environments? Can it still deliver benefits? Let's try to answer these questions.

Typical fixed scope projects are provided with a detailed specification document that is supposed to describe all the necessary details to provide a cost estimate. Sometimes the specification is also used by the development team to implement the application itself.

These specification documents are of varying quality. Some go into too much detail. Others skip blithely over complex functionality with barely a mention. It's not uncommon to see both shortcomings in the same document!

Nonetheless, the estimation team studies the document and associates a price tag (man-days, story points, etc) for each function. If the price is accepted, the team has to do the hard work: implement the application on the basis of the specification document, with the constraint of the attached price tag of the individual features.

A large portion of the work is about understanding the domain and trying to provide solutions for the requirements that satisfy the customer, stay within the scope of the original, contracted specification document, and stay within budget. There will be a lot of decisions (large and small) to make and, since the team is under the illusion that "everything was specified", they don't focus on documenting these decisions. These implicit and untracked decisions regularly lead to problems with change tracking and final acceptance.

In this situation BDD can help to provide a frame for domain discovery and for documenting the detailed requirement decisions the team makes.

One possible approach to achieve this is to use Example Mapping to prepare the individual features for development. Whenever the team is about to implement the next feature, they all study the related sections of the specification document and build an example map with all the rules and illustrative examples that they can discover. Once they have a better overview of the feature, they can match it to the expected budget and can then cut the scope if necessary. This is still very rough guesswork of course, but at least you have a better overview of the feature, so that you can make your cuts in a way that keeps the overall integrity of the feature intact. This might also include a couple of round trips to the customer, if possible. Once the scope decisions have been made, the team can progress with the development process, formulating the illustrative examples as scenarios that can drive the implementation of the feature.

As a result, you can transform the static (and probably already outdated) specification document into a continuously validated living document. This will not solve the problems introduced by the gap between the details described in the specification document and the details that are required to implement the application, but at least it will make the decisions explicit. Living documentation offers a way to track (and correct) decisions that turn out to have been wrong, as well as providing a mechanism for managing change requests.

Once you have gained the trust of the customer – and readable living documentation is definitely a big help with that – you will have a better chance to negotiate agile contracts with them later on.

4.6 - BDD in regulated environments

Operating in a regulated environment brings a higher level of expectation on traceability. The exact requirements and goals might depend on the concrete project, but generally the process should focus on the following areas:

- completeness and correctness of the specification
- coverage provided by the tests and the testing strategy in general
- evidence that the testing has been performed for a particular version

Behaviour Driven Development provides a combined representation of the specifications and the tests. Let's look at some important characteristics of the BDD process that might be relevant for these projects:

- The scenarios are selected initially to be illustrative examples of the specifications. The aim is to ensure consistency and shared understanding across the team.
- The set of scenarios can be extended by further test cases using the same format, to reach the coverage prescribed by the testing strategy.
- The scenarios are business readable and they bring together the specification and the tests. This duality ensures a higher consistency and linkage between these areas.

- The scenarios are strictly versioned, together with the application code.
- BDD tools typically execute scenarios directly and produce a report of the execution result.

These statements about the BDD approach show that it is not only a good foundation for projects operating in regulated environments, but the living documentation satisfies the regulatory requirements better than classic processes. The improved efficiency comes from the fact that the scenarios are business readable, so you don't have to maintain a separate document for the tests. The code and tests become self-documenting. If you run your automated scenarios and generate a report from the execution, this report will:

- document the expected behaviour
- describe the tests that have been used to verify the behaviour
- provide evidence of the execution results for a particular version of the product.

The report generation has to be well prepared in order to meet the formal requirements of the regulators. Even though the regulator will need additional documents (e.g. designs, architectures, state diagrams), BDD ensures that the most volatile part of the regulatory report is automated and integrated into the development process.

Agile practices are welcomed by regulators

The guidance on the use of agile practices in the development of medical device software (AAMI TIR45:2012[a]) has been published by the Association for the Advancement of Medical Instrumentation (AAMI). Since 2013 this report has been a part of the recognized standards[b] by the U.S. Food and Drug Administration (FDA).

The report addresses the usage of executable requirements in the regulated context (Section 3.6.5):

"The challenge comes with providing a reviewable requirements documentation package to regulators. A team must ensure the readability of whatever re-

quirements are pulled from the set of EXECUTABLE REQUIREMENTS. Use of formal, more English-like words in the requirements definition will facilitate this readability, as will the use of tools to package and organize requirements into a comprehensible outline.

EXECUTABLE REQUIREMENTS can be used as part of a final requirements documentation mechanism."

[a]https://my.aami.org/store/detail.aspx?id=TIR45

[b]https://www.federalregister.gov/documents/2013/01/15/2013-00605/food-and-drug-administration-modernization-act-of-1997-modifications-to-the-list-of-recognized

4.7 – What we just learned

BDD is a straightforward set of practices that, when combined, can significantly improve the quality of your team's development process. In this chapter, we expanded on the high level view of the BDD approach, to see the different activities that you'll work through. We looked at when each of these activities is suitable and which team members should be involved.

Because we understand that your teams differ, we looked at how BDD integrates with various common development methodologies and team configurations. There are more ways of working than Scrum and Kanban, but with an understanding of these you should be able to see how to adapt the BDD approach to your workplace. Whether you're working in a perfect agile fairyland or struggling with fixed price projects, you've seen how BDD can fit in.

We also discussed how, with appropriate technology support, BDD can work well for distributed teams, acting as an aid to collaboration. The unambiguous feature files act as a single source of truth that can ease the difficulties experienced when working across geographies and time zones, as so many of us do.

Every organization is different, though, so treat the approaches described in this chapter as starting points and refine them in your retrospectives until they fit your team perfectly.

Chapter 5 - How to get business involved

We have already explained how the most important element of Behaviour Driven Development is collaboration. Collaboration means that team members with different roles work together to deliver working software. A team will include both the business (product owners, project sponsors, business analysts, etc.) and technical personnel (such as developers, testers, UX experts and operation staff). It's a common mistake to focus just on collaboration between delivery team members.

In this chapter we would like to share our experiences of how to get business representatives fully involved in the BDD approach and what kind of challenges they might face. You'll see that we believe the key to successfully adopting BDD is to demonstrate to the business the value of collaborating with the delivery team. There is no fixed recipe for this – you'll need to develop and refine your strategy depending on your project context.

"The proof of the pudding is in the eating" – in the end, seeing the immense value that results from practicing real collaboration is the only way to demonstrate that BDD can work in your context. Our aim is to give your team enough enthusiasm to give BDD a try.

5.1 - Learn from you peers

The key benefits typically attributed to BDD are:

- reduced cycle time
- reduced rework/rejections
- reduced number of production issues
- keeping the implementation costs of new features under control

Although we provided reasoning that supported these benefits, nothing is more convincing than learning about existing projects that have applied BDD successfully. There are lots of excellent case studies in the book by Gojko Adzic "Specification By Example" [45], but it's even better to talk to people that have actually participated in a successful BDD project. The best place to meet these people is at conferences and user groups.

5.2 – The one where the business is not involved

Frequently, the BDD approach is introduced by the team or vendor that is responsible for delivering the solution. The business has probably not been involved in the BDD approach from the start. They might not have even heard of Behaviour Driven Development. In these cases, the team needs to find a way to "sell" BDD to them, by convincing them that their participation in this approach will help to deliver better results.

If you have ever tried to sell a new method or process to the business (especially one with a TLA – a three letter acronym), you'll know that this can be challenging. The business might:

- have a default resistance against new methodologies
- see this approach as an overhead
- be afraid of learning and infrastructure costs
- have formal or legal distance from the team (e.g. the business representative is a part of the customer, not the vendor)
- see BDD as a testing or a development technique

In some situations, teams might try to apply BDD without involving the business. This is sometimes called ***developer-only BDD*** or ***tester-only BDD*** and should be considered a Bad Thing™. A lot of teams and projects claim to practice BDD without involving the business and some of them seem to be happy with this. This is because

[45] Adzic, Gojko. *Specification by Example: How Successful Teams Deliver the Right Software.* Shelter Island, NY: Manning, 2011. Print.

collaborating at the development team level can still introduce clear guidance for how testing and test automation should be performed. Having this approach in place is better than an ad-hoc, chaotic testing strategy, but it does not deliver the massive benefits that are available by involving the business as well.

Seb's story: You Keep Using BDD, I Do Not Think It Means What You Think It Means

I've visited a lot of teams that don't have the business involved in "BDD". We have charitably described them as "developer-only" or "tester-only" BDD, but I tend to think of them as not following BDD at all. At best, they are using tools that were designed to support collaboration as expensive test automation platforms. The outcome is usually suites of automated tests that are slow to execute, hard to maintain and of limited value to the organization. They would get more value from dedicated test automation tools.

BDD is about collaboration. Using a BDD tool, or automating tests using *Given/ When/ Then* doesn't make your development approach BDD in the slightest.

Without the business involved, unless the team is very business-focused and disciplined, the scenarios become technical, data-driven and dry. This means that the business get very little value from reading the scenarios and, consequently, won't understand the implication of a failing scenario. This removes the possibility that the scenarios will provide a constructive feedback loop between the business and delivery team – so the scenarios become an overhead.

As we said earlier, the way BDD can "win" for the business depends on the project context. In some cases, the *developer/tester-only BDD* can be a step in this strategy. With the systematic, business-focused application of BDD, you can gather enough knowledge and examples, to demonstrate the benefits of BDD to the business, giving you a better chance of convincing them.

If you happen to be in the situation where you practice BDD, but your business is not involved (yet), consider the following advice:

1. Consider your situation as a temporary solution that you use as a step towards

full collaboration.

2. Think about your scenarios as business examples. Try to imagine how the business would explain the "story" behind the scenario. Use realistic data and business-readable phrases. Testers can be a big help in this, as typically they act as a mediator between the requirements and the solution.
3. Try to focus your detailed requirement discussions on examples. The business does not have to know that you're practicing BDD. "Could you please give a concrete example!" is a valid question in any process.
4. Present your results and methods to the business regularly and watch their reactions to figure out which aspects of BDD they find most useful. (Gaspar's story in Section 4.2, *BDD in Scrum* about showing scenarios in the sprint review is a good example of this.)

We've worked with many teams that initially resisted adopting a BDD approach because: "We cannot apply BDD, because our business does not want to be involved". You could try following a BDD approach without business involvement, as a first step – you'll get all the benefits outlined above and, in time, your business colleagues will come to appreciate the value of expressing the acceptance criteria as plain English scenarios.

5.3 – BDD is for solving problems

Once you are into the daily routine of BDD, you could explain it to your product owner in a way that highlights Example Mapping, formulation and automation. Or, you could explain the BDD as a process, as we did in Chapter 4, *Who does what and when.*

This might work for some people, however, presenting BDD in this way doesn't seem to be very appealing when talking to business team members. The problem is similar to one that we come across on a daily basis: focusing on the solution instead of the problem itself. BDD has no value unless it is helping you solve problems, improve development efficiency, and produce better results. In order to get your business colleagues engaged, you have to find the pain points (or opportunities) that exist in your current process. If there are no problems, and everything is just perfect, there is no need to introduce BDD.

Identifying these challenges is an important first achievement, from where you can build up sound justification for trying alternative approaches. It is impossible to enumerate all the different kinds of problems or challenges your project might face, but the following section provides a brief list of typical issues and the solutions that BDD can provide.

Product owner is overloaded

It might sound counter-intuitive, but BDD can help reduce the product owner's workload.

The lack of business availability is a common counter-argument to adopting BDD. "If they are already overloaded, increasing their level of collaboration would make them even more so.", is a typical response, but it doesn't have to be that way. Regardless of whether you use BDD or not, in the end the product owner has to provide the input that is needed to implement the application. Our goal with BDD is to improve communication efficiency by focusing on early, direct communication with the business, ensuring fewer misunderstandings and less rework. The following list compares the activities that product owners spend their time on in a BDD and a classic agile development approach.

BDD product owner activities

- participate in requirement workshops (e.g. Example Mapping)
- review the scenarios
- give feedback about the implemented application

Classic product owner activities

- writing specifications
- presenting the stories to the team
- discussing ad-hoc questions during implementation
- collecting deviations from the expected result in the Sprint review
- managing and prioritizing requirement-related bugs

If you compare the collaboration time needed from the product owner with the efforts needed in a classic development process, you can see that although BDD needs time spent collaborating and reviewing, we avoid re-discussing the same topics over and over again and the work is distributed throughout the team (e.g. scenarios written by the team will replace the written specification).

Production issues are common

Production issues are costly: as analyzed by an IBM study[46], the cost of a production issue is 30 times higher than "fixing" the same issue during the preparation phase. They are not only costly to fix, but they can easily result in customer dissatisfaction and mistrust.

In Section 1.3, *What about testing?* we described the relationship between BDD and testing: our goal is to prevent production issues being introduced during requirement analysis and detailed specification. The resulting reduction in production issues is the most easily measurable benefit of applying the BDD approach.

If production issues are common in your project, you need to take immediate steps to improve the situation. While the problem will probably need to be addressed from several angles, introducing BDD can certainly contribute to the ultimate solution.

It is hard to get the product to a deliverable state

There is a huge, frequently underestimated gap between implementing a feature and bringing it to a releasable state. There are a lot of "smallish tasks" you need to take care of, like creating deployment packages, updating user documentation or verifying performance requirements. Experience shows that these tasks are often deferred until the story (or release) is 'almost done'. Since the effort required for these activities is usually underestimated, the result is functionality that can be (partially) demonstrated, but still can't be released to the users.

To ensure that the application can be reliably released at short notice, the team should follow the ***continuous delivery*** (CD) approach. Continuous delivery requires the

[46]Briski, Kari Ann, Poonam Chitale, Valerie Hamilton, Allan Pratt, Brian Starr, Jim Veroulis, and Bruce Villard. *Minimizing Code Defects to Improve Software Quality and Lower Development Costs.* IBM, Oct. 2008. Web. ftp://ftp.software.ibm.com/software/rational/info/do-more/RAW14109USEN.pdf.

team to work on the application in short cycles, where each cycle contains all necessary steps to make the application deliverable. Since these cycles might be really short (often shorter than a day), a high level of automation is required to perform the necessary verification and packaging steps.

Seb's story: Delivery is not deployment

CD could stand for either *Continuous Delivery* or *Continuous Deployment* – these are not the same thing. Just because an application is in a deliverable state, does not necessarily mean that you will release it to end users. Whether a particular deliverable is released or not is a business decision, not simply a quality control decision.

The process that automatically builds, tests and packages each product increment as a potential deliverable, is called ***continuous delivery***. The process that also automatically releases each deliverable to end users is called ***continuous deployment***.

Continuous deployment is not necessarily applicable for all kinds of applications, but continuous delivery can be applied to all projects.

To move towards continuous delivery, stories should be sliced up into very small chunks. In Scrum the implementation of a feature or a user story is broken down to technical implementation tasks. Sometimes teams adopt an inadvisable approach called ***horizontal slicing***, where tasks are defined along the different layers of the application (e.g. "implement the data access layer for the story"). If the story is broken down in these ways, the application can only reach the deliverable state when all tasks are done and the entire story is finished.

The scenarios we use in BDD provide a *functional breakdown* of the story. Every scenario represents a part of the expected behaviour and makes sense on its own (***vertical slicing***). Even better, each scenario can act as a work unit (see Section 4.2, *BDD in Scrum*). If you routinely include the "smallish tasks" in the implementation of every scenario, you will keep the application in a releasable state. Now you're well placed to adopt continuous delivery or even continuous deployment.

It is hard to get customers engaged with the product

Nothing is more frustrating than delivering a good quality product that is not liked or used by the end users. While there are many reasons that cause this to happen, it can indicate a development process that does not focus on user value. You might be in this situation because your project organizes the work using *horizontal slicing* and ***technical stories***[47].

Since BDD encourages the team to focus on realistic examples of application behaviour, the product tends to evolve in line with the users' viewpoint. Also the collaboration techniques used by BDD can help UX experts get involved early in the design phase.

Deadlines are often missed

Deadlines, at least those ones you can miss, are set based upon an estimate of how long it will take to deliver the set of required features (the scope). However, as the name implies, estimates are just an estimation. They can be wrong... and often are. If the scope to be reached is fixed, there is not much you can do to meet the deadline if the estimate was wrong. You can force the team to work overtime, or you can allocate more staff, but these methods rarely provide an effective, long-term solution.

The key to the successful management of deadlines is to allow more flexibility in the scope: "Try to implement as much value as we can for the given deadline."

BDD will not tell you how to cut the scope, but it gives you a framework for enabling functional cuts, even within a user story. Scenarios provide a functional breakdown of the story, and give you the opportunity to reduce the scope by identifying and deferring lower priority behaviours when you are under time pressure.

Hard to get a good overview of the progress

Having a good overview of progress is essential to good project management. With a good overview, you have warning that meeting the deadline is in danger early enough to take action. Delivered scenarios are an excellent indicator of progress,

[47] http://www.innolution.com/resources/glossary/technical-stories

because you can track which behaviours are actually supported by the application. The traditional approach of calculating an arbitrary percentage of work completed, is not nearly as effective.

Introduction of new features causing unwanted side-effects

The success of a great new feature in the application can easily be overshadowed by a bug that gets introduced at the same time. And if a subsequent bug fix introduces two more defects, then all the excitement will vanish. As the code-base grows the chance of a change producing unwanted side-effects increases. This can lead to a seemingly endless increase in the implementation cost of new features. In the worst case, this can lead to a "rewrite-project".

Adopting BDD encourages good automated test coverage, where automated tests and scenarios are tightly connected to the requirements. Once a change causes a failing test, it is easy to diagnose whether this problem is related to contradictory requirements or defects in the code. The automated scenarios provide a useful safety net that protect you from unwanted side-effects and help keep the cost of implementing a new feature constant as the product evolves. Instead of being afraid to change the code, the development team is safe to experiment and see how the application reacts to them.

Not being able to react fast enough to market changes

In order to be able to catch up with the competitors, in a changing market, you have to establish a development model that keeps the cost of implementing new features low, while maintaining the quality of the application. Observing it from this angle, it becomes clear that the problem is closely related to the previous discussion of unwanted side-effects, so the same conclusions are also valid here.

Furthermore, we should also highlight that experiments are not only valuable at the code level (i.e. changing the code to see what happens), but also at the specification level. With the specification language you build up for expressing the scenarios, you have developed a framework within which the product owner or the business analyst can investigate how the system behaves with different parameters or different user workflows.

"Bug vs. feature" debates within the team

Too often, developers and testers build up their own solutions independently: the developers write the application code, the testers write the test cases. This redundancy might result in conflicts at the point when the two parallel worlds meet: when the test cases are used to test the application. These are the typical "Bug vs. feature" debates.

The rework and frustration caused by these debates can be avoided by reducing the redundancy and encouraging developers and testers to work on understanding the details of the requirements together. The collaboration demanded by BDD, and the scenarios that are the output of the collaboration (see Section 3.4, *Why stop now?*), help to improve this situation.

Changes regularly requested at the Sprint/feature reviews

The iterative development concept of agile is based on the fact that you can only get real feedback for a feature when business stakeholders actually get to see it in action. This is why we implement the application in small increments and this is why we organize Sprint/feature reviews.

While it is better to realize that the application is not doing exactly what it should at a Sprint review than realizing this after a two-year delivery cycle, fixing the application is still much more expensive than doing it right from the beginning. If you regularly discover changes during the review, you probably aren't discovering the detailed requirements well enough.

BDD supports the detailed requirement analysis in many ways. By focusing on examples, ambiguities can be recognized and cleared up (see Section 1.3, *What about testing?*). Additionally, since scenarios document the specification in the ubiquitous language, misunderstandings are less likely (see Section 1.4, *A language that is understood by everyone*).

But my product owner never reads the scenarios

A common situation is a product owner that never reads the scenarios. On closer inspection, this often turns out to be a symptom of a deeper problem.

Scenarios specify how the application should behave. If the product owner is collaborating in the creation of the scenarios, but does not seem to be using the ***living documentation***, you should check that they have access to the scenarios. Accessing files in source control is easy for developers, but is this how we want to publish our living documentation? Try to make it more accessible! There are tools available for converting plain-text feature files into a more readable form (see Section 1.5, *Living documentation*). Integrate the publishing process into the continuous integration pipeline and make the result easily accessible (by adding a link to the project dashboard, for example).

You might also need to consider how someone can find information within the living documentation. For instance, you might want to improve how you tag your scenarios, so that the information related to special topics can be easily found.

Even if you have an easy-to-access, nicely formatted document, it might take some time for the business to learn how to use it effectively. Be patient. Take time to regularly retrospect on how the living documentation is being used by the business and what changes might make it more useful.

Gaspar's story: When I first used Wikipedia

I still remember how I felt when I first heard about Wikipedia. It was hard to believe that an encyclopedia that is free and can be edited by anyone could be useful. So, I was a bit cautious in the beginning and did not trust the information I read. Over time I've learned when I can rely on the Wikipedia articles and when I should check other sources as well.

The situation with living documentation is similar to this. Everyone in the team has to learn how to use it and what questions can be answered with it.

Maybe more information is needed, such as an automation trace or a scenario change report. Perhaps a modified structure would help, such as organizing feature files hierarchically. Or possibly a different tagging policy, identifying the release that a particular behaviour was delivered in. Almost anything this is possible, you just need to talk together ;)

5.4 – What we just learned

BDD depends on collaboration. In this chapter we've emphasized how important it is to get the business involved in the BDD approach and looked at why this is sometimes difficult. We present some tips based on our experience of working with organizations adopting BDD, some of which may work for you.

The information presented in this chapter is broadly applicable, but you should also make use of other sources of experience within the software development community. User groups and conferences are good places to meet likeminded individuals and have in-depth, face-to-face conversations.

We will discuss the structure and content of good living documentation in detail in *The BDD Books: Formulation*[48].

[48]Nagy, Gáspár, and Seb Rose. *The BDD Books: Formulation.* In preparation. http://bddbooks.com/formulation.

What's next

You've made it to the end. Congratulations!

Thanks for reading this book – we'd love to hear what you thought about the book. If you have any suggestions, comments or a good story about your experiences, please write to us at feedback@bddbooks.com.

Where are we now?

In this book we've covered the first part of the BDD approach: Discovery. We've stressed the importance of collaboration, described workshops and techniques that can help your teams reduce misunderstandings, and illustrated this with our own experience in the software industry.

Our goal in writing this book was that it would be useful to everyone involved in the specification and delivery of software. So, please encourage the rest of your team to read it – it won't take long.

What's more is there?

This book covers the Discovery part of the BDD approach, but there's more to BDD than we have covered.

We haven't talked about the process of formulation (turning examples into scenarios) or other challenges you will face when working with large specifications. This will be covered (using Gherkin) in *The BDD Books: Formulation*[49].

Nor have we discussed test automation, which is often a major motivation for organizations looking to adopt BDD. We'll cover automating scenarios using SpecFlow in *The BDD Books: Automation with SpecFlow*[50].

---

[49]Nagy, Gáspár, and Seb Rose. *The BDD Books: Formulation*. In preparation. http://bddbooks.com/formulation.

[50]Nagy, Gáspár, and Seb Rose. *The BDD Books: Automation with SpecFlow*. In preparation. http://bddbooks.com/specflow.

How else we can help

Both authors develop and deliver training and coaching for organizations worldwide. If you would like to talk about the services we can provide, please get in touch at services@bddbooks.com.

Index

A

B

C

D

E

F

G

H

I

K

L

M

O

P

Q

R

S

T

U

V

W

Printed in Great Britain
by Amazon